W9-BAC-716

# Star
## style
### at the
*Academy Awards*

# Star Style

## at the

## Academy Awards

### A Century of Glamour

by Patty Fox
Foreword by Bob Mackie

SANTA MONICA

Photographs on preceding pages:

Whoopi Goldberg, 1994

Tim Robbins and Susan Sarandon, 1996

Meg Ryan, 1998

Kate Winslet, 1998

Elizabeth Taylor, 1987

Nicole Kidman, 1997

Clint Eastwood, 1995,

Catherine Zeta-Jones, 1999

Halle Berry, 1996

Mel Gibson,1996

Gwyneth Paltrow, 1999

Madonna, 1991

Drew Barrymore, 1983

AN **ANGEL CITY PRESS** BOOK

*Star Style at the Academy Awards*
By Patty Fox
Designed by Maritta Tapanainen
First Edition
1 3 5 7 9 10 8 6 4 2
ISBN 1-883318-14-9
Copyright © 2000 by Patricia L. Fox

Published in the United States by
Angel City Press. Inc.
Santa Monica, California
www.angelcitypress.com

The Oscar statuette design and the words "Oscar", "Oscars", "Academy Award" and "Academy Awards" are registered trademarks of the Academy of Motion Picture Arts and Sciences.

Library of Congress Cataloging-in-Publication Data
Fox, Patty
     Star Style at the Academy Awards : a century of glamour / by Patty Fox ; foreword by Bob Mackie.—1st ed.
          p.  cm.
     Includes bibliographical references (p. ) and index.
     ISBN 1-883318-14-9 (hardcover : alk. paper)
          1. Fashion—Pictorial works. 2. Costume design—Pictorial works. 3. Academy Awards (Motion pictures)—History—Pictorial works. I. Title.
TT506.F69 2000
391.2—dc21                              99-050544
                              CIP

Printed in Hong Kong

# DEDICATION

*To Bobby Cohn who introduced me to his world, Hollywood,*
*and shared it with all his love.*

Robert Cohn (second from right) and Alex Grassoff accepted Best Documentary honors for *Young Americans* from Diahann Carroll and Tony Curtis (right) in 1969.

# GRATITUDE

Some people in this world offer help even before they are asked. They are so loving and giving of their support, understanding and knowledge that an exhausted author is overwhelmed by their generosity. I have been lucky enough to work with such people on this project. First, my heartfelt thanks to Bob Mackie, Greg Schreiner and Tim Resar. Their special interests and incredible talents have contributed to the depth and beauty of this work. I shall always be grateful.

Surely a book about fashion at the Academy Awards presentation is not possible without the cooperation of the Academy of Motion Picture Arts and Sciences. My gratitude to Scott Miller, John Pavlick and Mikel Kaufman. And, without the staff of the Center for Motion Picture Study Margaret Herrick Library, this project would have been much more difficult. My sincere thanks go to Linda Mehr, Stacy Behlmer, Sue Guldin and especially David Marsh.

Knowledge gained from historical photograph specialists is invaluable when establishing the imprimatur of a book, giving it its unique identity. I am privileged to have worked with Carolyn Cole of the Los Angeles Public Library, Marc Wanamaker of Bison Archive, Dacy Taube of the Regional History Center of the University of Southern California Library and Lou Valentino.

Some folks are very talented at making connections and they never seem to get the credit they're due. Let these connectors be thanked: Don Adams, Fred E. Basten, Amy Inouye, Carlos Lamboy, George Marcelle, Tom McKinley, Nadine Ono, Sheila Perkins, Jane Putch, Katy Sweet, Tom Zimmerman. Carol Brodie and Dawn Moore of Harry Winston were enthusiastic supporters of this project from its inception. Laura Wenke graciously shared her knowledge and contacts in an industry where those are key gifts. My thanks too, to John David Ridge for sharing his personal experiences of stars and style.

As I was compiling *Star Style at the Academy Awards*, I was blessed to be associated with Project Angel Food's Divine Design. The team at Project Angel Food give of themselves every day and I am proud to have worked with them.

Congratulations and thanks to Maritta Tapanainen, whose artistry presented all the elements in this book with elegance.

Finally, there are loved ones who can never be thanked enough: my brother Bob Davis and his wonderful family, Susan, Jessica and Neil; and my dear friends Deborah Durham, Marian and Dick King, Mark McBride, Anne Ready, Lawrence Zarian and Alex Flores.

—*Patty Fox*

Paul Newman and Elizabeth Taylor, 1992

# Table of Contents

# Foreword

The Oscars started over seventy years ago as a little self-congratulatory party for the movie industry. Since then it has become the most terrifying, neurosis-making event of the year. The excruciatingly long show is watched by zillions worldwide and the one thing that everybody remembers the next morning is how fabulous or how hideous or how boring everybody looked. The gowns, the tuxes, the hair and the makeup are all up for discussion by the at-home, as well as by the so-called professional, critics. Everyone is fixated by movie stars and what they put on their backs.

I've been watching, working, and attending "The Oscars" for several decades and the pattern remains constant. The panic sets in and about a month before the ceremonies: "What am I gonna wear?" On occasion, the Academy has

In 1986, Cher presents Best Supporting Actor Award.

decided to set up a dress code for presenters. Well, you can imagine how that went over. Some people may like to be told what they must and must *not* wear but, of course, there are always the rebels and Hollywood is full of them. Actually, in 1986, the year Cher wore her infamous "Mohawk Meets Dracula" outfit, there was a printed dress code on what the well-dressed presenter should wear, and for some reason it didn't include feather headdresses and bare midriffs. Cher was a bit miffed by the fact she hadn't been nominated for her terrific performance in *Mask* and assumed that most of the voting members had dismissed her performance simply because she was "Cher" and couldn't possibly be a serious actress. So she just wanted to get really dressed up and have a great time presenting Don Ameche with his award. Well, guess who had all the coverage the next day? And guess whose outfit from that night is *still* being shown in magazines and newspapers all over the world? I've dressed Cher for seven Academy Awards and she always seems to get plenty of attention. People are always excited or at least curious about what she's going to show up wearing.

Of course I've dressed many normally glamorous people, too, over the years and there are always serious considerations to keep in mind when designing the dreaded Oscar dress:

1. Will her gown photograph well on TV and in still photos?
2. Will she look tall and thin enough?
3. Can she sit down?
4. Can she go up the stairs?
5. After sitting in the hot lights for hours, is she going to be a wrinkled mess?
6. Will her sweat stains show?

And don't forget…

7. Does she look good in the dress?

Now you know why we see so many basic black dresses at the awards.

Actually, the real show takes place backstage in the wardrobe department when hysterical presenters come running in with broken zippers, ripped hems, empty bodices that are promptly stuffed with bust pads. There is nothing like a hysterically nervous actress standing all but naked waiting to have her gown repaired minutes before she is about to be seen by the entire world. Because today's gowns are often delivered perilously close to show time, it can result in real fitting disasters. In the old studio contract days the studio designer would usually design the perfect gown and the actress would be fluffed and painted to insure the perfect and ongoing image of the studio's precious commodity. These days the kids are on their own. Everybody throws free clothes at them, which only adds to the confusion. This also makes for some very heated and ridiculous fashion discussions.

It's curious that no one has ever attempted a book on "Oscar duds" before. If the usual crazed fascination with what the stars are wearing is any indication, *Star Style at the Academy Awards* is destined to be a classic. Patty Fox and I

In 1984, Cher (above left) is nominated for Best Supporting Actress in *Silkwood* (1983). In 1988, Cher (above center) wins Best Actress Award for *Moonstruck* (1987). In 1998, Cher (above right) appears at the seventieth reunion of Oscar winners. In 1989, Cher presents Best Picture Award.

have crossed paths many times in our "clothing endeavors" and when she asked my opinion on some of the subjects while preparing her last book, *Star Style*, I realized this lady knows this town and how it thinks and how it dresses. She also knows all the intriguing and backstage stories from 1928 until now. Find out what makes the Oscar ceremonies the biggest fashion-watching event of this, and every, year.

—*Bob Mackie*

# Introduction

**S**ome people say there are only two ways to dress in Hollywood. One way is reserved for Oscar night. And no one really cares about the other way. Such is Hollywood. Stars who wear whatever they please the rest of the year, think twice about what they'll put on for the Academy Awards. In fact, most think for weeks. On Hollywood's biggest night of the year, the world is watching and no box-office-respecting celebrity wants to disappoint a billion viewers. Glamour—however a movie star may interpret that term—is the byword of the evening. As Miramax's Harvey Weinstein noted, "Clothes influence the movies, and the movies influence clothes. But these days, fashion seems to be what the Awards are for."

In many ways, Hollywood spent the last century of Oscar

Barbra Streisand, 1969.

nights building up to the fashion frenzy that exists today. It was no different in 1929, the year of the first Academy Awards ceremony; there were just fewer media types to blitz the world with who was wearing what. At the second Awards ceremony Mary Pickford sent off to Paris for her gown even before the official nominations had been announced. (There was no FedEx to allow for last-minute decisions, especially of the international kind.) And during the World War II years, despite an Academy ban on formal clothing, Hollywood's favorite gossip columnist was urging stars to rebel and go all out for the glamour. "After all," Hedda Hopper reasoned, "that's what the world wants to see."

Doubtless, early stars were as eager to look perfect as they collected their statuettes, as today's stars are. In Hollywood's golden era, costume designers who made the clothes for the hundreds of films that were released every year, helped dress the stars, putting a studio's stamp of approval on just about everything the stars wore in public. As celebrities became more independent, they took control of their offscreen wardrobes, and made their marks or faux pas on their own. By the 1990s Hollywood's glitteratti were sought after by the world's highest-priced retail fashion houses, companies all too cognizant of star power. When Mr. and Ms. Oscarfan can go to a designer's store the day after the show to buy the same thing their favorite screen stars wore, Oscar night is suddenly the biggest fashion show in the world.

Drew Barrymore, 1998

It's important to understand what it takes to dress for the Academy Awards. Not every star has style and that's why it was essential for the Academy to put a fashion consultant in place, early on. For many years, that was Paramount costume designer Edith Head's job. The queen of design—who reigned in Hollywood from 1921 until her death sixty years later—sat at the edge of the Oscar stage, making certain that too much cleavage wasn't showing, that skirts weren't too short (she missed a mini one year) and to help stars who might otherwise look ordinary (she artfully stuck a rose in Grace Kelly's French twist just before the future princess walked on stage, so her exit would be as beautiful as her entrance). But as times changed, so did tastes. Head was replaced by many different masters of cloth—including her onetime protégé Bob Mackie—until 1989 when Fred Hayman, the retailing maestro of Rodeo Drive, took over.

Hayman showcased high fashion. He opened the doors of his Rodeo Drive clothing store to celebrities who needed guidance about dressing for the Academy Awards. They would schedule appointments and either find the perfect ensemble

Kristin Scott-Thomas, 1997

on the rack or meet with designers who would custom-make the perfect look. He staged fashion shows with more than thirty models to give nominees and presenters (and the world!) trend advice—it was he who declared that pastels would be hot in 1999, weeks before the biggest stars all turned up in sugar-coated colors. He can take credit for much of the excitement that is now generated by Oscar fashion.

And so can the stars. What would the Academy Awards be without Cher challenging the limits of the censors and of Mackie's imagination? Or without Geena Davis outdoing herself each year? Or Jodie Foster, finding in her conservative manner, Armani's most extraordinary style? Or Whoopi Goldberg, expressing herself as only she can? "I don't usually do trains," she'll tell you as she swishes off, "But, Honey, this is the Oscars."

*Star Style at the Academy Awards* is devoted to the artists who have created the art of Academy Award fashion, be they the wearers or the designers. It is not about bad fashion—about tennis shoes ungracing a stage, or tuxedos worn backwards, or gowns that overpowered their stars—but, rather, very good fashion. *Star Style at the Academy Awards* is about fashion that has made a memorable statement for its star. Bette Davis, Audrey Hepburn, Elizabeth Taylor and Geena Davis have all earned a feature of their own in these pages. *Star Style at the Academy Awards* is about the incredible jewels celebrities have chosen to wear, about the children who have presented themselves so well, about the men who gave tuxedos style, about the celebrities who knew how to reach back into history and find style that lasts for decades.

To understand this amazing extravaganza of international design, it helps to look at the Academy Awards over time, to see the origins of its style, the impact of the studios, of the stars who put their signature style on stage, and, finally, of the designers who use stars as their mannequins. This book is divided into four parts, each of which explores one of those emphases. Dates credited to Academy Awards ceremonies in this work refer to the year of the films being honored, unless otherwise specified. Thus, when Vivien Leigh was nominated for Best Actress for 1939's blockbuster, *Gone with the Wind*, and wore a printed gown to the 1939 Academy Awards ceremony, she was actually wearing that glorious formal in 1940 when she accepted her statuette. Likewise, when Gwyneth Paltrow appeared in a pink gown in 1999, the last woman to win the Best Actress award in that century, she was attending the 1998 Academy Awards ceremony. Such distinctions will cause confusion in Hollywood research circles forever.

No matter what the date, however, glamour has never escaped Oscar's stage. Some years have been more glamorous than others, but nothing can separate Hollywood from glamour. And nothing broadcasts star style better than the Academy Awards.

—*Patty Fox*

Winona Ryder, 1996

# Origins of style

**H**istorians don't talk about what Janet Gaynor wore to that very first Academy Awards banquet in 1929, the year she took home the golden statuette for Best Actress. Visionary she was not. Had she already married costume designer Adrian, it might have been different, but the gown was never mentioned. The next year's winner, Mary Pickford, shrewd businesswoman that she was, started planning the gown she would wear to accept her trophy several weeks before she had finished filming her Academy Award vehicle, *Coquette* (1930).

Silk chiffon was Pickford's chosen cloth: a diamond brooch anchored the draping bow on the fitted torso that defined her delicate bustline, yet didn't distract from the bead-encrusted hip yoke atop the long bias-cut skirt that skimmed her little toes. Her arms were heavy with sparklers, too: a diamond ring and dramatic bracelet on the left arm, a slimmer band of rocks on her right arm. She topped it all with a maribou feather-trimmed wrap. So it was when America's Sweetheart took home the second Academy Award for Best Actress.

Pickford, the prescient film mogul and actress, knew exactly how powerful the Awards she helped institute would become. She knew that the fabled glamour of Hollywood was what appealed to the public, what they craved. Pickford anticipated that America would soon be completely aware of who won what, and yes, indeed, who wore what. Gaynor admitted that she didn't have a clue: "Had I known then what winning an Academy Award would come to mean in the next few years, I'm sure I would have been overwhelmed."

At Awards ceremony in 1930 with Conrad Nagel, Norma Shearer wore the gown that Adrian, the MGM costume-design legend, had created for her film *The Divorcee* (1930). She noted to him, "People will see me holding the Academy Award in the very same dress I wore in the film and say 'How very, very appropriate.' "

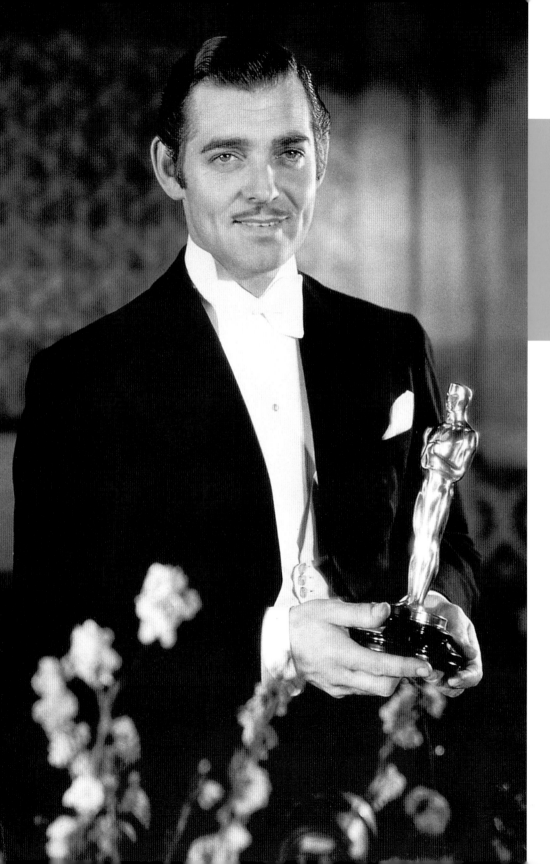

In 1935 at the seventh Academy Awards banquet, Clark Gable received his only Best Actor Oscar for *It Happened One Night* (1934), dressed formally in white tie.

Although the public rejected Mary Pickford's first talkie, *Coquette* (1929), Hollywood's only female mogul knew that earning an Academy Award for Best Actress would rekindle moviegoers' interest in the film. So as a founding member of the Academy of Motion Picture Arts and Sciences, she engineered a win. In fact, several days before the actual announcement, dressed in the finery she had been planning for months, she posed for this photo, featuring the coveted gold statuette. Her commanding stance in this photograph by George Hurrell showed the business-woman side of America's Sweetheart.

At the Awards ceremony in 1934, Best Actress nominee Diana Wynyard, who starred in Fox's *Cavalcade* (1933), was called to the speakers' table by the host of the evening, humorist Will Rogers. He kissed her and then announced that Katharine Hepburn, who was out of town, had won the Award. Though many wondered why Rogers called her forward, Wynyard's glorious satin evening gown undoubtedly provided the kind of elegance that furthered the grand image Academy producers envisioned for the ceremony. She's flanked by her *Cavalcade* co-star Clive Brook (left), Fox executive Winfield Sheehan (center) and director Frank Lloyd.

Norma Shearer, the third Best Actress winner, connected with Pickford's glamour strategy and wore a mink-sleeved gown Adrian had designed for her role in MGM's *The Divorcee* (1930). In succeeding years, Marie Dressler came draped in ermine. And, although Helen Hayes opted to wear a simple black gown, she was gilded in pearls, diamonds and a cascading corsage that reeked of a 1930s superstar.

It wasn't until the advent of televison coverage of the ceremonies in 1953 that America fully appreciated the Oscar show as one huge fashion show. Until then, what the stars wore to the event was strictly the stuff of movie magazines and gossip columns, tales told after the fact to titillate and

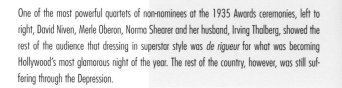

Shirley Temple was asked at the last minute to give Claudette Colbert her Best Actress statuette, since no one had expected the actress to attend. Colbert's excuse? She was on her way to New York for a well-deserved vacation. She appeared only after the Academy's publicist Leroy Johnston reportedly turned up at the station to announce her win. "I'll miss my train and I'm not dressed," she responded. His comment that "It's the Nobel Prize of motion pictures" convinced her to delay the train and head to the ceremony for a six-minute appearance. Although the publicity machine at the Academy said the whole event was absolutely spur of the moment, how remarkably lucky that she came from the station wearing that gorgeous corsage on her lapel.

One of the most powerful quartets of non-nominees at the 1935 Awards ceremonies, left to right, David Niven, Merle Oberon, Norma Shearer and her husband, Irving Thalberg, showed the rest of the audience that dressing in superstar style was *de rigueur* for what was becoming Hollywood's most glamorous night of the year. The rest of the country, however, was still suffering through the Depression.

Gail Sondergaard and Walter Brennan (left) were the first actress and actor to be awarded for their supporting performances in a film. Despite the photograph, Sondergaard didn't win a statuette for her part in *Anthony Adverse* (1936); instead both she and Brennan received plaques to commemorate their accomplishments. They're shown here with George Jessel, the host of the evening. Accepting her award with sheer flower power, Sondergaard looked as if she blossomed in 1967, not 1937.

executives made certain that the other nominees, Diana Wynyard and May Robson, were on hand that evening). It would have been a bigger problem the following year since Claudette Colbert, star of America's favorite movie *It Happened One Night* (1934), was boarding a train to New York at Awards banquet time. As the legend goes, she was not expecting to win, so when her name was announced as Best Actress, her train was delayed at Union Station. Colbert, in her traveling suit and fur, was ushered to the nearby Biltmore Hotel to make a six-minute appearance, and then rushed back to get back on board.

The following year Bette Davis showed up at the Awards wearing nothing dressier than an afternoon frock to accept her gratuitous Best Actress award for *Dangerous* (1935) and executives at her studio, Warner Brothers, were furious with her. That plain dress was Davis' way of thumbing her nose at the Academy after Colbert won the 1934 Oscar. Davis' performance in *Of Human Bondage* (1934) was one of best and

amuse. If pictures circulated, they were few and quite late. Those early gowns were the subject of Saturday morning beauty shop conversations; maybe there was a Vogue pattern that a talented seamstress could use to whip up a similar style at home. But who but a movie star had the need for a long gown? These were the stuff of dreams.

Studio heads, Pickford included, were determined that their stars feed those dreams. Their plans were inhibited at the 1934 banquet when the twenty-three-year-old Best Actress Katharine Hepburn didn't show up to accept her statuette (so

The De Mille cousins, Agnes (left) and Katherine (center), carried on the family tradition of opulent style wearing jewels and fur to the 1936 Awards ceremony. The De Milles are on the arms of director Mitchell Leisen, who had been a costume designer and set decorator for the Katherine's father, obviously had a flair for style with his dapper Dali-esque moustache. Actor Tom Brown and actress Ida Lupino (resplendent with her mink muff) complete the stylish fivesome.

resulted in numerous write-in votes for her by Academy members. (When Davis lost, a controversy ensued over the number of votes she had actually received, and Price Waterhouse was retained to count the secret ballots the following year.) Not only did the press complain loudly about her plain dress, but Jack Warner lectured her and she was dutifully gowned the following year when she was scheduled as a presenter.

Davis was to become a frequent face at Academy Awards ceremonies, nominated ten times throughout her sixty-year career. Her style was as diverse and dynamic as her roles, causing comment whenever she appeared. Unlike her con-

temporaries Joan Crawford, Marlene Dietrich and Carole Lombard, Davis wasn't comfortable using sex appeal as a tool—she wanted her talent to reign supreme. Plus she was never comfortable with her looks, especially compared to the likes of Lombard, Dietrich, Luise Rainer, Merle Oberon and some of the other ravishing leading ladies of her day. She learned to make the most of her looks, learned her fashion lessons from Hollywood's best teachers and her career outlasted those of every glamour girl.

Shirley Temple capped her initial year as a mega-star, albeit at age six, as the first child actor to be recognized with a special Academy Award. Her trophy, a miniature of the gold statuette adult stars received, acknowledged her "outstanding contribution to screen entertainment during the year 1934." Though her stardom was never to be duplicated by another child, many youngsters were later recognized for their talents, including Judy Garland, Mickey Rooney, and Margaret O'Brien, who was only four when she appeared in *Babes on Broadway* (1941) and seven when the Academy named her Outstanding Child Actress for her performance in *Meet Me in St. Louis* (1944). In modern days it is no longer a surprise to see a child nominated for an Award, but it was news in the first decade when the likes of Temple and O'Brien lit up the screen.

The pattern that was set during the first decade of the Academy Awards ceremonies established a demand for glamour. Among both men and women there was no doubt that this was the night for stars to shine, for photographers to click, and for the public to get a glimpse of what Hollywood was meant to be. As the Awards ceremony itself gained recognition, the medium for the glamour message was fashion. The pageant that would last into the next century had begun.

Legend has it that Luise Rainer was at home wearing her slippers when her name was announced as winner of the Best Actress Award for her role in *The Great Ziegfeld* (1936). Meanwhile, downtown at the Biltmore Hotel where the ceremony was going on, Gladys George, another nominee, had overheard in the press room that Rainer had clinched the Award and tearfully gave the news to fellow nominee Carole Lombard. They both bemoaned the fact that studio politics would ensure that Rainer would win the next year for *The Good Earth* (1937) which, indeed, she did. Studio executives insisted that next time she wear something a bit fancier than this monastic crepe gown with its draped neckline and long sleeves (the only dress she had handy when she received the call from Louis B. Mayer to "put on some makeup and get downtown").

# Bette Davis

BETTE DAVIS HAD BEEN NOMINATED for ten Academy Awards when she died in 1989. Although she had always thought the number should have been higher, her appearances at the Awards ceremonies were as talked about as her roles. Initially satisfied to just be herself at the event ("I dress for myself," she was known to say), she quickly learned that making a statement paid off.

Wearing what she called "a simple but pleasant dress" to accept her first Best Actress Award in 1936, was a critical fashion faux pas, a mistake she had to admit after being chastised by studio executives and criticized by her adoring movie magazine editors. She tried a more glamorous approach the following year and looked only slightly better than matronly. By 1939, however, the first of the five consecutive years that she was nominated for Best Actress, she came to the Awards dressed to be remembered, in a gown by Colette bedecked in egret feathers and jewels. "The movie magazine editors had told me that housewives across the country expected glamour from an actress, and they had a point, for it was still the Great Depression."

At the Awards banquet in 1941 which was broadcast on radio, she publicly thanked President Roosevelt for addressing the group by telephone. Wearing a simple, bare-shouldered black dress, she noted "I never dreamed I would be on the same bill as the President of the United States." Her career took a downturn in the 1950s, when strong-willed, powerful women so popular in the war years were suddenly out of

vogue. In 1955 she appeared as presenter of the Best Actor award to Marlon Brando. She startled the audience by wearing a sequinned and jeweled gold helmet since her head had been shaved for her role as Queen Elizabeth I in *The Virgin Queen* (1955).

Back to the screen in the 1960s, her crumbling face was perfect for roles in the decade's popular shocker genre, but her image at the Academy Awards events continued to be one of the glamorous screen queen she had been. When she was nominated as Best Actress for *Whatever Happened to Baby Jane?* (1962) she wore a low-necked, but otherwise reserved gown reminiscent of her *All About Eve* (1950) costume. Since she was already "an old-timer," as one newspaper syndicate called her, she wisely had adjusted the shoulders to be less revealing.

Whether in the first decade of her career or the last, acting was her art and fashion was a marketing tool to help further her creative pursuit. Always shrewd, she knew that what she wore to the Academy Awards would translate to dollars at the box office. By learning early to make star style work for her, she ensured her status as one of Hollywood's most enduring stars. ◆

1955                    1937

1941                                        1939

Shirley Temple's first year at the Academy Awards was not just to receive her Special Award for her contribution to the film industry, but also to present Claudette Colbert's Best Actress trophy. Her success as a child star lasted about as long as her ringlets; by the time she was twelve she was a box-office flop. Obviously America loved the storybook looks of the wonder child who could, at age six, hold an audience in the palm of her dimpled little hands. Despite the fact that she grew into a beautiful ingenue, no one could forget her as Curly Top, Rebecca of Sunnybrook Farm and Heidi. A grown-up Shirley was too much to accept.

Judy Garland was bussed by her best beau, Mickey Rooney, when she received her career's only Oscar statuette, albeit a miniature version. In 1940 she was recognized for her contributions as a juvenile star after her role in *The Wizard of Oz* (1939). Wrapped in rabbit fur, she looks every inch the star clutching her trophy in her tiny white gloved hands.

# Children and Oscars

SHIRLEY TEMPLE MADE NINE FILMS in 1934 and to the chagrin of most of the other leading females, she was undoubtedly the biggest dollar draw at neighborhood theaters. She was the reason parents could take their kids to the cinema, she was prolific and, of course, she was gorgeous. But unlike a few years before when Little Jackie Cooper at least had been nominated as Best Actor for his role in *Skippy* (1931), she was overlooked when it came to nominations. Not about to shock America, the Academy issued a Special Award, a miniature statuette, recognizing her achievements that year. Suddenly a child was in the ranks of Charles Chaplin, Warner Brothers and Walt Disney, the only other Hollywood types who had been specially recognized by the Academy.

When she appeared at the front table to collect her trophy, it was presented by the playwright, novelist and actor Irvin S. Cobb, who told her "When Santa Claus brought you down Creation's chimney, he brought the loveliest Christmas present that has ever been given to the world." The words were long forgotten, but the image of *Little Miss Marker* (1934) holding her mini-Award with ringlets in perfect place and pleated skirt only slightly askew, lived on in every movie magazine in America.

Bob Hope had to lift eight-year-old Margaret O'Brien to speak into the microphone when she received her special award in 1944, the year she appeared in four movies, most notably *Meet Me in St. Louis*. Deanna Durbin, Mickey Rooney and Judy Garland would be

among several young people recognized by the Academy until 1960 when Walt Disney's *Pollyanna*, Hayley Mills garnered the last special award for juvenile acting.

By 1962, sixteen-year-old Patty Duke took Best Supporting Actress honors for playing the young Helen Keller in *The Miracle Worker* (1962), a role she had created on Broadway. Just as significant, she

Margaret O'Brien had lost her front teeth by the time the Academy was ready to give her a Special Award for her talent. So her studio, MGM, insisted that she wear the same false teeth to the Academy Awards that she had worn in *Meet Me in St. Louis* (1944). No matter that they gave her a Bugs Bunny smile. "My apprehension was that one of the false teeth …might fall out, as they often did when we were making the film," she recalls. She once admitted that she had a crush on host Bob Hope, so meeting him at the Oscars was a treat. "He even hugged me; he hugged most of the other actresses, too, but I was the only one he both hugged and lifted." Another failure in adolescent roles, O'Brien tried to make comebacks, but was never the success she had been at age seven holding her mini-statuette.

was competing against another child actress, Mary Badham, of *To Kill a Mockingbird* (1962), who was nine, and three adults. On the night of the Awards, Duke looked prom-ready in her organza-and-satin evening gown and teased hairdo, both of which were far too matronly for the still-baby-faced teen. When little Tatum O'Neal copped the Best Supporting Actress Award for her role in *Paper Moon* (1973) at ten years of age, she was the youngest person ever to win an Oscar. And, of fashion importance, she was undoubtedly the first female to appear in a man's tuxedo at the illustrious event. Anna Paquin was also named Best Supporting Actress well before she reached her teens, and wore a beaded-and-crocheted beret to take

"She was only ten years old, but she knew exactly what she wanted…She was a woman in a child's body," explained costume-designer Nolan Miller, who created the tuxedo that Tatum O'Neal wore when she picked up her Best Supporting Actress Award for her role in *Paper Moon* (1973). Inspired by seeing Bianca Jagger wearing a tux, the youngest Academy Award winner in history captivated her audience with her fashion daring.

As she accepted her 1993 Best Supporting Actress Award from Gene Hackman, Anna Paquin became the second-youngest actress to win an Oscar, and wore an ensemble her mother made of iridescent silk taffeta.

Poor Patty Duke. She had to grow up so fast that when she received a well-deserved Oscar for Best Supporting Actress, she looked far older than her seventeen years. Her face still had a tomboy youthfulness, but her Windsor-like ensemble, complete with Queen Mother shawl and handbag, reflected her lost youth, a child-star who was forced into maturity too soon. Duke was escorted to the event by her pet Chihuahua.

"Yo quiero Oscar," as Patty Duke's Chihuahua Bambi might say. Duke took him with her to the Academy Awards in a bowling bag the night she was honored.

home her Oscar for *The Piano* (1993). Her "it's pretty cool" response to winning the Award won hearts, and her beret started a short-lived trend among the junior-high set.

From the earliest Shirley Temple days, young thespians have brought a certain style to the Academy Awards ceremony. It was indeed a style that worked when the children looked their age—but when stage mothers got in the way and turned their children into mini-grownups to appear at the Awards, the result was fashion disaster. ◆

# Studio style

"The ermine, mink, silks and satins that constituted the femme finery for the occasion represented an investment of better than half a million dollars," read *Daily Variety* the morning after the Academy Awards celebrating the films of 1939. Considering the contenders, glamour was essential that night, even though the *Gone With the Wind* star Vivien Leigh was a shoo-in for Best Actress. Nominees Bette Davis (*Dark Victory*) and Greer Garson (*Goodbye, Mr. Chips*) both attended the ceremony at the Coconut Grove. The other contenders, Irene Dunne and Greta Garbo stayed home, obviously not women enough to

Vivien Leigh looked ready for a Tara barbecue when she attended the 1940 Academy Awards in this bold floral print gown—all she needed was a straw sun hat. She was a ravishing standout in a sea of solid color sheaths glittering with rhinestones, sequins and beads. Until then, no Best Actress winner had worn a print dress, except Bette Davis in 1935, who was duly criticized for the frockishness of her choice; Leigh was betting on this gown getting positive reviews.

face a loss. Or, perhaps, they just couldn't decide what to wear.

Leigh attended, swathed in white ermine and escorted by her fiancée Laurence Olivier and her producer David O. Selznick. Inside the Grove, she shed the fur and looked a bit like a modern-day Scarlett O'Hara, in her full-skirted, floral print gown. She eschewed Walter Plunkett's extreme sleeve detailing, however, and opted for spaghetti straps that revealed as much skin as decency would allow. Nestled in her cleavage was a huge faceted stone so clear that her skin shown through. At her wrist was an antique bracelet laden with colored gems. Her face wore the confidence of a winner.

Until the *Los Angeles Times* leaked the results early, Olivia de Havilland wore the gleam of victory too. Everyone thought she would beat Hattie McDaniel, who was, after all, black, for Best Supporting Actress. The consensus was that McDaniel's win had come in simply being nominated: no black actor or actress had ever achieved such recognition. So

Ginger Rogers took her Number One fan—her mom Leila—with her the night she was nominated for Best Actress for *Kitty Foyle* (1940). Ginger Rogers was dressed to the nines, partially in support of Hedda Hopper, who had beseeched stars to defy the Academy's lock on glamour and dress with true star style. As Hopper asked, "Would it break down anyone's morale to see our grils beautifully dressed?"

Selznick Studios wardrobe mistresses draped a boa of gardenias from Hattie McDaniel's shoulder to her waist to adorn the simple dress she wore to the 1940 Academy Awards banquet. More significant than her nomination as Best Supporting actress was that she was the first black woman to ever be nominated for any Award. Stunned by her win, she broke into tears after her acceptance speech.

McDaniel, who was draped in gardenias, had memorized a speech written by a studio publicist and broke into tears when she concluded it. Olivia de Havilland broke down, calling the evening "a learning experience."

The night was also an extraordinary fashion night because Frank Capra, as Academy president, had sold the rights to Warner Brothers to make a documentary of the ceremonies. Studios had instructed their stars to go all out in the dress category, knowing that this short film would be shown in theaters all over the country and promote the glamorous image of the industry. Only two years later the mood had changed. After President Roosevelt saluted the industry's

Studios taught their stars that winning an Oscar pushed them to another level of stardom; winning was worth all the dollars and energy that could be put toward the goal. They neglected to say that the benefit went to the studios in those days, since the stars were under contract and their salaries were locked in. After an Oscar win, the fee other studios paid to "borrow" a star, known as a loan-out fee, escalated. As an example, Joan Fontaine (above left) was making thirteen thousand dollars a year under contract to David O. Selznick at the time she won her Oscar for *Suspicion* (1941), but other studios paid Selznick two hundred thousand dollars to use Fontaine in a film after her Best Actress Award. Such was the power of the Oscar. The public reinforced the message by flocking to films that won Oscars. It behooved the studios to force the stars to maintain the glamour image. Fontaine, still making thirteen thousand dollars a year, was forced to maintain her glamorous wardrobe, have a race horse, drive a fancy car and have a huge house with servants, all to further her mythic image. In this photo, she got off easy, since the Academy had gone on its wartime austerity campaign and asked stars to dress conservatively. Fontaine took austerity to an extreme and came dressed in a black mantilla, usually reserved for mourning, to accept her Oscar at the 1942 ceremony. Ginger Rogers looks on.

Ginger Rogers was not about to disappoint a soldier. She sat with her husband Private John Briggs II at the Academy Awards and gave him a glimpse of the Hollywood glamour that his contemporaries relished the pinups. The 1943 Awards ceremony was particularly patriotic, featuring a message from President Roosevelt, and Privates Tyrone Power and Alan Ladd as flag bearers. Despite the Academy plea for austerity, Rogers wore what she knew the soldiers wanted to see.

it was with fanfare and emotion that Fay Bainter presented the Best Supporting Actress Award to her with the following words: "It is a tribute to a country where people are free to honor noteworthy achievements regardless of creed, race or color."

Ingrid Bergman wore the same dress to the 1945 Oscar ceremony that she wore in 1944, the year she and Jennifer Jones were competing for Best Actress honors. When Jones won the race for her performance in *The Song of Bernadette* (1943), her acceptance speech contained a public apology to Bergman, who had been nominated for *For Whom the Bell Tolls* (1943). Backstage, Bergman replied, "No, Jennifer, your Bernadette was better than my Maria." Jones wasn't nominated in 1944, but when Bergman took Best Actress honors, the pair celebrated together. As this photo taken at the 1945 soiree shows, Bergman was typically without much makeup—one magazine reported that "she never so much as carries a compact."

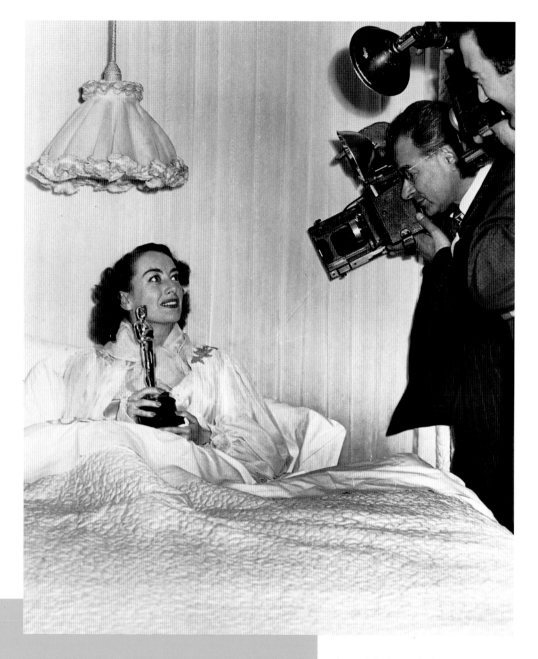

She had worked herself up into a 104-degree temperature, as legend tells it. Joan Crawford was photographed at home, in her four-poster bed, accepting the 1945 Best Actress Award for *Mildred Pierce,* in her favorite peignoir (designed by MGM's Helen Rose, of course), which just happened to be handy.

patriotism speaking by telephone at the 1941 Awards, when Pearl Harbor was bombed in December of that year, there was talk of canceling the next Awards ceremony completely. Early in 1942, however, cooler heads had prevailed and the Awards were slated for February twenty-sixth. Rather than the splashy banquet and dance format of the past, the 1942 event was a more somber evening. No dancing, no formal dress. Women were asked to make donations to the Red Cross instead of wearing flowers. Even the Oscars were made of plaster. Austerity was the byword.

Gossip columnist Hedda Hopper was angry at the Academy's ban on formal wear and led what she called a "guerrilla war of my own to doll up the Academy Awards, when the studio chieftains still wanted the presentation to look no dressier than a missionary's sewing bee." She waged her campaign for four years, telephoning the stars directly, telling them to celebrate in true star style. "Last year you looked like spooks: sackcloth and ashes," she chastised. "But nobody's going to be dressed," the stars replied to Hopper. "Then set the style. What are you going to do? Let those clothes rot in your closets?"

Most women followed the Academy's dictates, however, and wore knee-length dinner suits or simple dresses and hats. Joan Fontaine, for example, came draped in a black mantilla secured with two roses to accept her Best Actress Award for *Suspicion* (1941). Even Loretta Young, known for her flamboyant, impassioned sense of style, attended the 1942 ceremony dressed simply with her only nod to glamour coming from a pillbox hat covered in faux pearls. Ingrid Bergman, perhaps the most conservative of all, wore the same dress two years in a row when she was nominated for Best Actress.

When the war ended, so too the dearth of glamour. The white ties and sparkling dresses were back. In 1946, the Best Actress was Joan Crawford who had made herself sick from her fear of not winning. She and renowned publicist Henry Rogers had begun the first public relations campaign to garner a nomination well before she had completed filming *Mildred Pierce*. The pressure on her was so intense that when the big night arrived, she was paralyzed with fear of rejection and couldn't get out of bed. The relentless Rogers took advantage of the drama, and gathered press photographers at her home. When her name was announced, she rushed for her best peignoir, a spritz of perfume and a face full of makeup. She was camera-ready by the time director Michael Curtiz arrived with her Oscar. The resulting photographs were so bizarre that editors all over the country solely featured Crawford on their front pages.

That peignoir had been designed by MGM's studio costume designer, like most of the clothes stars wore to further their images. MGM's Helen Rose, Paramount's Edith Head, Warner's Orry-Kelly and Columbia's Jean-Louis were instrumental not just in the costumes of the movies, but for everything their stars were photographed wearing. Yet until the late 1940s, these behind-the-scenes wizards went totally unnoticed (except for Head, perhaps, who was a master at self-promotion). Led by Head, the designers united to demand that their work be recognized with an Academy Award. In 1948 the Award for Costume Design was established and awarded to Dorothy Jeakins for the color film *Joan of Arc* (1948) and Roger K. Furse for the black-and-white film *Hamlet*. Head was crushed about losing (however, her next thirty-five nominations and eight wins would make up for it).

At one point in 1948, when postwar interest in movies was on the wain, rumor had it that the Academy was going to fold, since cost-cutting measures at the studios weren't leaving dollars to subsidize the gala dinner and ceremony. *Time* magazine chastised the industry for abandoning the singular Hollywood event to which the public could relate, leading its story with the headline "Little Orphan Oscar." In a last-ditch effort, crafty Academy president Jean Hersholt promised the studios that he would use studio starlets as presenters, giving their careers a boost. The offer worked. In fact, it was a young

When she took the Best Actress Award for *To Each His Own* (1946), Olivia de Havilland selected a strapless, hand-painted gown and accessorized it with nothing more than a choker of little pearls.

After Fredric March presented her the Best Actress Award for *The Farmer's Daughter* (1947), the totally surprised Loretta Young admitted that she was relieved that she had selected a dramatic emerald green silk taffeta gown. "Up to now this event has been a spectator sport. But I dressed, just in case." For many years, the Oscar she won resided in her guest coat closet in her front hall, situated on a shelf all by itself, with the automatic door light shining down on it. "Every time I open the closet...I'm delighted all over again to be chosen a winner."

Elizabeth Taylor who presented the new Costume Design Award. (The next year, starlet Marilyn Monroe noticed that her dress was ripped just before she went on stage, burst into tears and had to wait for a wardrobe mistress to sew her back together.) Although the Academy survived, the year 1950 was the worst in the history of the film industry. Box-office dollars dropped to their lowest levels, no single new film or new star had yet captured the public's heart, and worst of all, from the industry's perspective, Americans were beginning to watch television.

Hersholt's successor, Charles Brackett, decided to join forces with the enemy and use it to full advantage. The Academy Awards presentation was televised on March 19, 1953, and the show had the largest audience in television's then-short history. Coincidentally, sexy Marilyn Monroe was almost single-handedly bringing America back to the movies as the prosperous Eisenhower years gave the public both dollars and leisure time. What fun it was to watch the "Oscars" and then head to the movies.

Despite her disappointment at losing that first Oscar, soothed by winning the next two in succession, Head accepted an appointment as official fashion consultant to the televised Academy Awards ceremony in 1953. "I was appointed guardian of hemlines and bodices," she quipped. Before the big evening, NBC had advised nominees and presenters to avoid wearing white because the lights would cause a glare. Head would help the stars choose pale colored gowns and shirts, beforehand. Then backstage, she was actually charged with making certain that the stars were dressed appropriately

to pass the uptight television censors. She was on hand to put roses in décolletages that were revealing too much bosom and spray a dimming film on diamonds that sparkled too brightly. "We couldn't trust the stars who were to go on stage," Head recalled. "After I approved their gowns, some would push up their cleavages just before going on." In 1958, Edith and everyone else involved in the show got a memo from producer Jerry Wald stating "There will be no cleavage on this year's Oscar Awards show. This was one of the major criticisms we received last year, that the necklines were too low. Most of the

America viewed Jane Wyman as a deaf-mute in *Johnny Belinda* (1948) the same year she divorced the future President of the United States, Ronald Reagan. A banner year, no doubt, as she was nominated for Best Actress for the role. She elected to wear a slim, figure-revealing sheath that draped at the hip. Her friend Loretta Young opted for spangles and lace that evening.

Lovable Lucille Ball presents the Short Subjects Award to Cedric Francis, who accepted for Robert Youngman, for the one-reeler *World of Kids* (1951). She's dressed a la Lucy Ricardo.

This rare photo of Marilyn Monroe in her only Academy Awards ceremony appearance belonged to the famed actress. Dressed in black tulle, she presents the 1950 Best Sound Recording Award to Thomas Moulton for *All About Eve* (1950).

In 1955 Grace Kelly was not yet a princess, except in the hearts of America's movie fans. Kelly called winning a "numbing experience…I wanted to win so badly that I was afraid I would stand up no matter which name was read out." Edith Head designed the silk spaghetti-strapped gown that Kelly wore with a matching evening coat. Head lied blatantly to the press about its origins: "The material alone cost $4000 because the rare color could be achieved only by dyeing individual threads before the fabric was specially woven in Paris. She will be in blue champagne." The glamorous gown was Head's revenge, since she had to put Kelly in the trappings of a dowdy wife of an alcoholic singer for her Oscar-winning role in *The Country Girl* (1954). Edmond O'Brien took the Best Supporting Actor Award for *Barefoot Contessa* (1954).

In 1958, Sophia Loren presented the Best Director Oscar to David Lean for *The Bridge on the River Kwai* (1957) wearing a brocade sheath that emphasized her voluptuousness.

Dorothy Dandridge attended the New York branch of the Oscar ceremony in 1955, wearing a slim sheath, draped gracefully at the hip. She presented the Best Film Editing Award to Gene Milford. She was also nominated for Best Actress for *Carmen Jones* (1954), up against Grace Kelly in *The Country Girl*, Judy Garland in *A Star is Born*, Audrey Hepburn in *Sabrina* and Jane Wyman in *The Magnificent Obsession*. In the late fifties, she was the first African American actress to be cast twice as a leading lady, following up *Carmen Jones* with *Porgy and Bess* (1959).

Ingrid Bergman presents a Special Award to James Baskett ("Uncle Remus") who was the only live actor in Disney's animated feature, *Song of the South* (1947). Her draped gown with classic Grecian lines and her natural hair style were unlike other dolled-up stars of 1948.

complaints came from the middle west. If you need any help, a wardrobe mistress backstage is equipped with enough lace to make a mummy."

By the mid-fifties the television show had become not just an Awards show, but a long-awaited fashion show with the "supermodels" of the day: Elizabeth Taylor, Grace Kelly, Lana Turner, Marlene Dietrich and Audrey Hepburn. Talk in newspapers and magazines centered not just on the winners and losers in the various film categories, but the winners and losers in the fashion race. Press agents and studio wags started taking advantage of the fashion opportunity. They'd create sagas about gowns: Joanne Woodward sewed her own gown one year, Lana Turner was going to look like a mermaid, Vera-Ellen was going to dress in tight gold lame to look "like Oscar, himself."

Many actresses started wearing gowns to the Awards that

Eva Marie Saint presented the Best Supporting Actor Award to Jack Lemmon, who played Ensign Pulver in *Mister Roberts* (1955). Saint had been named Best Supporting Actress the year before in Columbia's *On the Waterfront* (1954). Her peplumed gown, with bridal buttons on the torso, looks very slim, considering she had just had her baby Darrell a day after the previous ceremony.

Accompanied by Humphrey Bogart (third from left) and resplendent in a patch-work silk taffeta ballerina-length dress, Lauren Bacall (second from left) was nominated for Best Actress for *Written on the Wind* (1956) at the 1957 ceremony. Her co-star, Robert Stack (second from right), attended with his new bride, Rosemarie, and took Best Supporting Actor honors. Microphones are set up in the foyer of Hollywood's RKO Pantages as television cameras and interviewers cover the stars' entrance.

Her role as Robert Stack's sex-hungry little sister in *Written on the Wind* (1956) earned Dorothy Malone an Oscar for Best Supporting Actress. Her taffeta gown featured a portrait neckline, perfect for jewels. She chose to go without.

No one expected Joanne Woodward to win the Academy Award for Best Actress in *Three Faces of Eve* (1957), least of all, Woodward. Everyone had their money on Elizabeth Taylor for *Raintree County* (1957). "I didn't invest a lot of money in the dress—I was convinced nobody would see it." Indeed, she spent one hundred dollars on the fabric and designed it herself. She had to hold up the front of the strapless gown as she dashed down the aisle to collect her statue. "I'm almost as proud of that dress as I am of my Oscar." That bitchy Joan Crawford said "Joanne Woodward is setting the cause of Hollywood glamour back by twenty years by making her own clothes." The clever Woodward countered a few years later, wearing a stunning Bill Travilla gown, "I hope it makes Joan Crawford happy." Above, Woodward and Paul Newman (right) presented the Best Film Editing Award to Peter Taylor in 1958.

were similar to gowns they had worn in their films. That was a reflection of what was happening on the streets of America. Women were dressing like their favorite movie stars. They quickly bought the copies of the white crystal-pleated dress Monroe wore in the *Seven Year Itch* (1955) originally designed by Bill Travilla. The Chinese *cheong-sams* that took an Oscar for defining Jennifer Jones' character in *Love is a Many Splendored Thing* (1955) were instantly adopted as party garb, even on the PTA circuit. The black, bateau-necked gown that Givenchy designed for Audrey Hepburn in *Sabrina* (1954), later became the design for the most popular prom dress in America. And the lace dress she wore that year to accept her Academy Award for *Roman Holiday* was a foreshadowing of the style, making the look all the more desirable. As a salute to costume designer Orry-Kelly, who was later overlooked for an Academy Award nomination for *Auntie Mame*, Rosalind Russell came to the 1957 ceremony wearing the beaded pajama ensemble she wore in the film. "It was rather daring of me, I admit, but after all, there is just so much you can do with women's clothes at an affair like the Academy Awards...I decided to try a complete departure," quoted Russell.

Both Elizabeth Taylor and Audrey Hepburn also provided their own form of departure from the norm at the Academy Awards ceremonies they attended. They were the biggest stars of the decade and they were each determined to make a huge impact on the fashion scale, too. Taylor's style was to showcase her body and her jewels. Hepburn brought a unique definition to the word beauty, and introduced Givenchy as one of the first important designer names to be linked to the Academy Awards. That was indeed one of the rare instances of foreshadowing in real life, a sign of things to come.

In 1958, Lana Turner presented the Best Supporting Actor Award to Red Buttons for *Sayonara* (1957). Nominated for Best Actress in *Peyton Place* (1957), Turner came to the Awards event accompanied by her mother and daughter, not her notorious boyfriend Johnny Stompanato. When she got back to her hotel that night, she was savagely beaten by the mobster who was angry at not having been her date. Ten days later he was murdered and Turner's daughter was charged, but acquitted. In her autobiography, Turner said she felt like a mermaid in that Oscar gown and recalled the "incredible contrast of the evening."

# Elizabeth Taylor

THE ACADEMY WAS STILL placating film studios by featuring starlets at the Awards show when seventeen-year-old Elizabeth Taylor presented the first Costume Design Award in 1949. The most beautiful teenager in America looked like a piece of wedding cake in her ballgown with its pouffed skirt and forget-me-nots strewn from dropped-shoulder to hem. She had just broken up with her first real boyfriend, Glenn Davis, but he escorted her to the Governor's Ball anyway. She pleased him by wearing the pearls he had given her in sweeter times.

Taylor would be squired by many different escorts to the Academy Awards over the years, wear many elegant gowns and exhibit many examples of her favorite avocation, jewelry collecting. Her appearances at the Oscar show were numerous and despite the fact that her personal life was tumultuous and often considered immoral, she has always been greeted by throngs of adoring fans. They loved her through every husband, every hairstyle, every body shape. A woman that beautiful, they rationalized, had the God-given right to have men falling at her feet.

Her first husband Nicky Hilton had already fallen and been kicked aside by the time Elizabeth appeared for the second time on the Oscar stage in 1954, this time with a new cropped hairstyle and an over-designed satin and lace gown with a wide chiffon swath at the bosom. She teamed with her new husband Michael Wilding to present the Oscar for Documentaries to Walt Disney.

When she was firmly entrenched in her third marriage, she went to the Oscars as Mrs. Mike Todd, producer extraordinaire. The diamond tiara was fitting for the Queen of Hollywood, since he was certainly the King, having just won the Best Picture Award for his film *Around the World in 80 Days* (1956). She also presented the Best Costume Award, her shirred chiffon gown befitting the task. Though she was nominated the following year for Best Actress in *Raintree County* (1957), Todd's fatal airplane crash four days before the ceremony cast a tragic shadow over all Hollywood. The young widow stayed at home to mourn.

She attended the 1958 Awards with her soon-to-be husband

1993                    1951

Eddie Fisher, even after Hedda Hopper and most of Hollywood berated her for having "not mourned enough"—to which Taylor retorted, "Mike's dead and I'm alive." As if to thumb her nose at her detractors, she wore a black dress—indeed, a sexy chiffon number, revealing her by-then-famous cleavage—to present the Writing Awards and to be passed up for Best Actress for *Cat on a Hot Tin Roof* (1958). The Oscar would elude her for a third year in a row (she was nominated for 1959's Best Actress honors for her role in *Suddenly, Last Summer*), but she was there dressed in an angelic white chiffon gown.

1976                                    1959

When her Best Actress award finally came, she was dressed in a Christian Dior gown. It was pristine, especially compared to the provocative garb she wore in her Oscar vehicle, *Butterfield 8* (1960). The crowd wasn't focused on what she was wearing that night, however. They were rejoicing that La Liz had recuperated fast enough from a tracheotomy to appear. Her legs were still so swollen after the surgery, however, that Burt Lancaster had to help her stand at the podium to accept her long awaited trophy.

She was separating from Fisher just about the time that the 1961 Awards were being announced. And since she was on location for *Cleopatra*, falling in love with Richard Burton and had neither been nominated, nor asked to present, there was no need for a special gown in 1962. In fact, she wouldn't return to the Oscar stage until 1970 when she was asked to present the Award for Best Picture of 1969. For weeks gossip columnists had been reporting that she would actually wear the sixty-nine-carat diamond that Burton had given her. Though it showed off the jewel well, the lavender-blue gown designed by Edith Head was mostly forgettable. It was a toss-up whether the diamond or Taylor's extraordinary beauty got more attention that night. Four years later, the marriage had ended, and the diamond had gone into cold storage. She came back to the Oscars, this time to present Best Picture of 1973. The Valentino gown she donned was muumuu-esque in a vibrant floral print, typical of the times, but less than flattering. The Burtons' remarriage and another divorce left America wishing that they hadn't seen Liz in that dress.

Not one to be defeated by her mistakes, Taylor bounced back in 1976, wearing what might have been the most beautiful dress of the Oscar's century. The strapless Halston gown draped at the bosom and fell to the floor in a long column of Elizabeth Taylor Red, as the designer named its perfect shade. Not even the University of Southern California Marching Band that surrounded her on stage could take away her command of the crowd.

Taylor appeared at the Awards three more times in the twentieth century, dressed by the likes of Hollywood's Nolan Miller and Valentino. Her style never let her fans forget, that she was The Star of Hollywood's first hundred years. ◆

1949                1967

# Diamonds and Oscars

SHIRLEY TEMPLE POSED WITH THE 756-CARAT uncut Jonker diamond in 1934, her lips pursed in an "oooh!" Harry Winston had made the first commercial connection between Hollywood and diamonds. Then in 1944, Oscar nominee Jennifer Jones was reported to be sporting a diamond necklace and earrings borrowed from the famed Fifth Avenue jeweler. It was the first time a jeweler loaned diamonds to a star for the big night. By the end of the century, every star who was nominated for an Academy Award received a congratulatory note from Harry's son, Ronald, as well as an invitation to view the newest sparkling collection. No star need go to the affair without some rocks.

And few miss the opportunity to sport multiple carats of ice. Stars and stylists line up at fine jewelers' showrooms prior to the big night, or welcome representatives bearing jewels into their homes. Oprah Winfrey, for one, refuses to borrow gems, however. She wears her own. Likewise, Elizabeth Taylor, who made headlines around the world in 1969 when she wore the 69.42-carat Taylor-Burton token of Richard Burton's love as a pendant (she sold it after their second divorce for close to three million dollars). Joan Crawford, enamored of diamonds throughout her career, also voted to wear her own gems, a blatant symbol of her enormous success.

It's a given: celebrities wear diamonds. And why not? The sparkle connotes stars and that's the Hollywood message point. To be noticed, wear diamonds. That's exactly what motivated Taylor to become a diamond collector, and Crawford, Gloria Swanson, even Mary Pickford. The association is old, but it never loses its appeal.

Throughout the century stars have continued to use the Oscar stage to help create the more-than-subliminal link between diamonds and success. Unfortunately, when the party's over, most of the gems go back to the store with their bodyguards. Of the stars who are trusted to keep the gems overnight, "nine out of ten will admit to me in a shy whisper that they slept in them," says a representative of one of the most prestigious houses.

Best Actress Norma Shearer displayed multiple diamond bracelets in 1930.
Celine Dion wore the Chanel comet necklace in 1997.

Presenter Angela Bassett wore more than seven million dollars worth of diamonds to the 1996 Awards, including a two-hundred-seventy-carat diamond necklace from Harry Winston.

Joan Crawford wore the same diamonds to the 1962 Academy Awards ceremony that she had worn in the 1940s. The dramatic jewelry is actually a necklace with a detachable brooch. Decades before, she had worn the brooch to a restaurant, lost it and it was tossed into the trash by a busboy convinced that something that large couldn't be real. It was found; he was fired.

The Taylor-Burton diamond, as it came to be known, deserved a dress designed by Edith Head. Elizabeth Taylor wore the gown and the sixty-nine-carat pear-shaped diamond in 1970, when she presented the 1969 Best Picture Award. Her then-husband Richard Burton was nominated for Best Actor for *Anne of a Thousand Days* (1969) and didn't win. In 1979, the diamond sold for nearly three million dollars.

The fifteen-carat blue diamond necklace worn to the Oscars by Best Supporting Actress nominee Gloria Stuart was worth twenty million dollars, and required that she have two security men with her at all times. *The Titanic* (1997) star told a reporter, "The necklace goes back tomorrow: but I'm keeping the bodyguards."

The seventy-one million dollars worth of rocks that Whoopi Goldberg flaunted at the Awards show in 1999 were simply a facet of her personal style. She had been cultivating her knowledge of diamonds ever since the Jim Henson puppet Miss Piggy donned gems on television. "If the pig is going to wear diamonds, the Whoop is going to wear diamonds," Goldberg asserted.

For the purveyors of diamonds, having a star seen in their jewelry on Oscar night equates to thousands of dollars of advertising, sometimes millions. In the case of the $490,000 necklace Celine Dion wore in 1997, Chanel reported that the necklace sold immediately after she appeared on stage wearing it. The French fashion house judged that Dion's association with that necklace was equivalent to nine million dollars in advertising. Realizing the potential, the next year, Dion donned diamond-studded Ray-Ban in exchange for the company making a fifty thousand dollar donation to her favorite charity.

Jewels on loan make a different statement about a star than jewels for keeps. In the heyday of Hollywood, stars such as Crawford, Marlene Dietrich and Gloria Swanson wore their own treasures over and over again, the way Winfrey and Taylor do. Owning their own jewels was regarded by the stars and the film studios as a status symbol that would leave fans in awe. Maybe it's time for stars to start following the lead of Oprah and Liz, and start buying their own gems again.

Famed Beverly Hills jeweler Martin Katz joked with Emma Thompson about the four carat diamond stud earrings she borrowed from his collection the night she won her Best Actress Oscar. He offered to trade them for her statuette. In true star style, she declined. ◆

"When is a girl going to wear a tiara if not to the Oscars?" asked Salma Hayek who donned a tiara at the 1996 Awards show.

One of the few stars who refuses to borrow jewels, Oprah Winfrey has worn her own diamond necklace to the Oscars on more than one occasion, in the tradition of Hollywood's classic stars.

1954

# Audrey Hepburn

IT WAS MARCH 25, 1954. The girl with the big eyebrows and long neck had just rushed crosstown from the 46th Street Theater where she was appearing in *Ondine*, to the Century Theater where she was about to change her life. In the dressing room she washed the stage makeup off her face and ran her fingers through her bangs. She donned the lace dress with the bateau neckline that would go down in history. She added little teardrop earrings. When she was called to the stage, Fredric March handed her an Oscar for being the Best Actress of the year in *Roman Holiday* (1953). And, by the way, the British Film Academy had just announced the same thing across the Atlantic. "This is too much," she said.

She would be nominated four more times as Best Actress, and was called into service as an Award presenter many times. Each time she appeared she was dressed by Givenchy. "Hubert de Givenchy has always dressed me—professionally and in private life," she wrote in 1990, "in a certain way one can say that Hubert de Givenchy has 'created' me over the years."

Givenchy's influence came to the public's attention when Edith Head received the Academy Award for the costumes in *Sabrina* (1954). Head gave a courtesy nod to Givenchy in her acceptance speech, but never told the whole truth: that he had actually designed the gowns that became Hepburn's signature. (Givenchy was so polite that he waited until after Head died in 1981 to tell the world that, indeed, he had created the historic "Sabrina" dress).

Givenchy also got notice that year for baring Hepburn's clavicles in a simple shoulder-strapped evening gown. It was a big night for the young star who was nominated for a second time as Best Actress for *Sabrina* (though she didn't win), and was asked to present the 1954 Best Story and Screenplay Awards. The following year, charged with presenting the award for Best Picture of 1955, Hepburn

1967

appeared on film, since she was working in London.

Her image of innocence and fragility was always reinforced when Givenchy shaped a simple white gown for her appearance presenting 1960's Best Picture Award to Billy Wilder for *The Apartment*. The following year, when she was nominated for Best Actress for *Breakfast at Tiffany's* (1961), Hepburn should have been wearing yet another "pretty dress" from Givenchy and major diamonds from Tiffany that she brought with her on a plane from Switzerland. But instead of attending the ceremony, she spent the evening in bed at the Beverly Hills Hotel with a bad cold, and had to watch television to see Sophia Loren take the Best Actress honors for *Two Women* (1961).

In 1965, she was the only major player in *My Fair Lady* (1964) *not* to be nominated; Academy politics had surfaced, since half of Hollywood was irritated that Hepburn had the lead in the film version of the role Julie Andrews had played on Broadway. So despite her fine lead performance, no nomination. The film's producer, Mervyn LeRoy was outspoken about the situation, "I find it very mean of Hollywood not to have nominated this great actress." With her typical guts, she attended the Awards ceremony to present the Best Actor Award, as a replacement for the 1963 Best Actress, Patricia Neal, who had recently suffered a stroke.

"Givenchy outfits gave me 'protection' against strange situations and people because I felt so good in them," she once said. Her armor for this stressful night was angelic white satin, with the neckline high enough to cover any indication that she was dramatically underweight. Elbow-length white gloves and diamond-and-emerald drop earrings were her only accessories. As it turned out, she presented the Award to her *My Fair Lady* co-star Rex Harrison. So with his black tails and her classic, unadorned white gown, they looked as if their attire had been orchestrated by Cecil Beaton, the film's costume designer whom Hepburn once had described as "a schoolboy imp."

By 1967, Hepburn and Givenchy needed a break from the white gowns she had been wearing to the Oscars. The designer and his muse created a pale green metallic one-shouldered topped with a luminous, long, lean evening coat, which she shed to present the Best Picture Award to the producers of *A Man for All Seasons* (1966).

It was back to white, however, the next year. She was nominated for Best Actress in *Wait Until Dark* (1967), and was also presenting Best Actor again. Givenchy's creation was a glittering vest, secured with a bow, worn over a long white skirt. In her typical style she went without a necklace, even though she had opted for a low neckline. Not afraid to accent her long neck, she rarely took the classic approach of breaking the line with jewelry.

Although she had been among the world's favorite actresses (along with Elizabeth Taylor, Shirley MacLaine, Doris Day and Marilyn Monroe) in 1960, Hepburn was absent from Hollywood and, thus, the Academy Awards, throughout most of the seventies. Except for two visits to the Awards, one in a stunning strapless black gown to present the 1975 Best Picture Award for *One Flew Over the Cuckoo's Nest*, and another in 1979 when she donned a red-and-black dotted dress to present an Honorary Award to King Vidor, her fans had very little opportunity to observe the changing face and style of Audrey Hepburn in the seventies.

Hepburn attended the Oscars only three times after that. Givenchy was determined to keep her shoulders bared throughout the years she was

1988

1968

aging, as if to tell the world that Audrey Hepburn was indeed ageless. In both 1985 and 1991 he opted to expose one shoulder, first in a pink sari, then in a regally draped red gown that she topped with a white coat. In 1988 when she and Gregory Peck teamed to present the Writing Awards, her black-and-white strapless gown was covered with coin dots and trimmed with stripes.

She was scheduled to appear at the Oscars one more time, in 1993, to receive the biggest honor of all, the Jean Hersholt Award. But a couple of days after she learned she would receive it, she died. It was fitting, some thought—from the first time she hit the screen, the world viewed her as an angel. ◆

1976

1992

# Signature style

**E**lizabeth Taylor and Audrey Hepburn appeared on the same Oscar stage, wearing virtually the same dress in 1961. Hepburn's was utterly French, by Hubert de Givenchy. Not to be outdone, Taylor's was equally French, by Christian Dior. Hepburn's was sleeveless, high-necked, sashed at the waist and full skirted. Ditto for Taylor. The only difference was the stuffing. There was no mistaking Taylor's voluptuous curves; the dress was filled to its comfort level. Hepburn's gown bagged on her slim body, no crinolines for extra shape. They were the yin and yang of fashion, at a time when the country was about to learn what yin and yang meant.

In 1961, *Los Angeles Herald-Express* dutifully reported that, dressed by Beverly Hills designer Don Loper, Shirley Jones looked "like Cinderella in a gold and white full-length bouffant gown with beaded bodice, beaded jacket and matching gold beads in her hair." She and Peter Ustinov took Best Supporting Actress and Actor Awards for *Elmer Gantry* (1960) and *Spartacus* (1960), respectively.

They were also the symbols of the end of the Golden Years, the demise of Hollywood's studio system. The leading ladies had become more powerful than the studios that had launched them. Along with Doris Day, Shirley MacLaine and, of course, Marilyn Monroe, these brunettes were sizzling at the box office. If any two women could be independent and create their own look in a town dependent on cookie-cutter beauty, it was Hepburn and Taylor. As glamour icons they could open the door for new stars to present signature styles, images that would be theirs and theirs alone.

The 1960s were ripe for independence as well. Film studios were forced to recognize independent film makers as solid competition, foreign films were attracting dollars at the box office, and stars were refusing to sign binding contracts. Actors and actresses wanted to control their roles, their careers, their incomes. Surely they would control their own closets. At the same time, Americans had cast off the

Julie Christie accepted her Best Actress Award for *Darling* (1965) wearing the shiny gold jumpsuit by Don Bessant, looking too much like the Award itself. Other actresses have come dressed like the statuette, including Farrah Fawcett-Majors in a metal mesh halter gown in 1978, Susan Sarandon in a metallic Calvin Klein in 1993, Ellen Barkin in Versace and Madeline Stowe in another shiny Calvin Klein, both in 1994. As early as 1959, Vera-Ellen wore a form-fitting gold lame sheath. "Why not?" she asked, "It's the way Oscar himself dresses!"

cloth-coat conservatism of the Nixon years, and elected a new president whose stylish first lady shifted the fashion focus from sewing bees to shopping sprees. As history had taught in the 1920s, a good economy raised hemlines considerably. Teenagers were listening to Brian Hyland sing about that "Itsy Bitsy Teeny Weeny Yellow Polka-Dot Bikini," opening eyes to public displays of a sometimes-innocent bareness that had never been acceptable before. The times, indeed, were changing and changing fast. Fashion was the visual gauge of the changes that were occurring.

Shirley Jones and Sophia Loren both collected their Oscars on Academy Awards night in 1961 and 1962 wearing gowns that suited the image of the classic movie star. Pouffy skirts, dripping with froufrou; beautiful, yes, but decidedly of another era. The stars were caught in the recent past, somewhere between grande dame garb and passé starlet style. The new guard was accepting the sleeker silhouettes that would reign for the remainder of the century. Ann-Margret was the unpredictable trendsetter in 1962 in her chic skintight gown, singing a nominated song, the title theme from *Bachelor in Paradise*. Her provocative persona was the winner, however, not the tune. The "sexy cupcake" image (as the *Los Angeles Times* called it) that she created for the Academy stage, garnered so much press that she would maintain it throughout her career. And the

sleek look would become the symbol of Oscar fashion for years to come.

Compared to the fashion world's runways that were promoting up-to-there miniskirts, the Academy's shows of the mid-sixties were relatively tame. Julie Christie, whose film *Darling* (1965) had showcased the mini, eschewed a short skirt, and appeared on the Oscar stage wearing gold pajamas. Edith Head, still the show's official fashion consultant, was

Wearing a kimono-style gown by Dorothy Jeakins, who was costume designer for *The Sound of Music* (1965), Julie Andrews was nominated for Best Actress for that film and presented the Best Actor Award to Lee Marvin for *Cat Ballou* (1965).

Just elected governor of California, Ronald Reagan and the state's new first lady, Nancy, spoke with the Academy's red carpet host, Army Archerd. Although neither former thespian had attended to accept an award, their attendance exemplifed the growing political importance of Hollywood.

Barbra Streisand, in what *Women's Wear Daily* writer Chauncey Howell called "a nice pink bar-mitzvah-mother dress" with a matching pillbox hat, presented 1969 Best Actor Award to John Wayne for *True Grit* (1969).

Nominated for Best Actress for *Pillow Talk* (1959), Doris Day elected to wear a two-piece gown Hollywood designer Irene created for the Awards. Day later wore the same design in *Midnight Lace* (1960).

nonplussed: "How did I know she was going to get dressed up as an Oscar until she got up on stage? Some people are just so independent that you expect them to dress differently." Although she had chickened out at the 1966 awards show, Christie was not about to miss the opportunity to create a sensation the following year when she presented the Best Actor trophy. Defying the Academy's ban against miniskirts, she snuck past Head's censoring eye and arrived at the podium wearing a polka-dot chiffon mini dress with a dropped blouson waist. Her hemline was a full two feet shorter than the maxi worn by British actress Wendy Hiller, who accepted for Paul Scofield.

But Christie's exposed legs didn't cause the fashion commotion that Barbra Streisand's exposed derriere did in 1969. Yes, her shapely buns were covered by fabric, but fabric that became translucent when the harsh TV lights turned on. "Shocking" was all Head could utter. Only a few years later a streaker topped Streisand's almost-nude appearance by running starkers across the stage as the audience and host David Niven just stared in disbelief. The guy was arrested; Streisand wasn't. The popularity of Gerome Ragni and James Rado's musical *Hair* (1968), with its famous onstage nude scene, had loosened the rules of propriety a bit—so as long as Streisand was covered, no matter how loosely she defined that word, she deemed herself appropriate. After her exposure, it seemed that the new theme song for the Awards show was "Anything Goes."

Best Actress of 1972 Liza Minnelli gets bussed by her co-star Joel Grey, who took Best Supporting honors and Al Ruddy, who produced the year's Best Picture, *The Godfather*. Ruddy was far out in his shiny tux, Grey was conservative and Liza was simply chic in Halston cashmere. Her op-art dog collar and starry-eyed lashes were part of her signature style.

And so it did. Elizabeth Taylor exposed so much cleavage cushioning the diamond Richard Burton gave her that everyone forgot that he didn't win an Oscar that night for *Anne of a Thousand Days* (1969), his fifth and last nomination without a win. At the same show, Candice Bergen wore an Arnold Scaasi poncho to present the Best Song Award and Streisand showed up in a demure pink dress accessorized with a matching pillbox hat. Ali MacGraw's hippie fringed vest over pants was a tribute to all the love-children who were too busy turning on to tune in that night. The Oscar show had suddenly turned from Hollywood's most glamorous night of the year to its most rebellious.

The stars of the 1970s would force Oscar to get hip. Self-expression appeared to be every major celebrity's goal as they paraded the stage. No longer would the classic mold of movie star work. Marlon Brando officially rejected his Best Actor award by proxy, a woman in full Apache dress. Diana Ross wore a silver tuxedo with a rhinestone vest, and little Tatum O'Neal donned a black tux. Katharine Hepburn showed up in her tattered gardening togs to present the prestigious Irving Thalberg Award. Cher bared most of herself in a multi-colored chiffon bra top and sarong. Jack Nicholson presented the Best Picture award wearing a colorful Polynesian-print shirt and a McGovern for President button. Stars were making statements. Their own.

There was one undeniable fact: fashion was getting more interesting than the long, boring Awards show. Indeed, show

producer Howard W. Koch had to admit, "The marketing surveys showed us that people actually care more about the clothes than who wins. So we are paying strict attention to giving the public what it wants." Prescient as always, the too-chic designer Halston of the Studio 54 set in New York showed up in 1976 like an answer to Koch's prayers. The top

Hippies had been influencing fashion since Haight-Ashbury days, but it was Sonny and Cher, the love couple of 1968, who brought long hair and sandals to the Academy stage. His damask Cossack suit and Cher's braids and barefoot sandals were more flower power than the Oscar audience had ever witnessed.

By 1974 the sixties' supermodel Twiggy had become an actress and was offering an Oscar to Edith Head for her costume designs in *The Sting* (1973). Her bib-front peasant dress with leg o' mutton sleeves and lace headwrap was in sharp contrast to Head's Chanel-esque vest-and-pants ensemble.

American name in fashion, Halston put his imprimatur on the Oscar ceremony—as he sat in the audience to watch both Elizabeth Taylor and Jacqueline Bisset wear gowns he designed. Yes, fashion was in the rarefied air.

Halston got an eyeful that night. There was Taylor, elegant in his red strapless gown as she led the audience in singing "America the Beautiful." And Lily Tomlin, looking quite like Cinderella, decked out in a silver lame gown, white fox fur and the cheapest little tiara ever to grace a Best Supporting Actress nominee's head. Jack Nicholson kept on his Ray-Bans throughout the evening. Ulla-Britt Soderlund, costume designer for *Barry Lyndon* (1975) accepted her Oscar in an eighteenth-century getup replete with tricorne and heart-shaped beauty spot. Lee Grant elected to go to a used-clothing store to find a vintage gown. It was quite a fashion show.

From then on, anything went. Over the course of the 1970s Sylvester Stallone appeared with open shirt and medallion. Diane Keaton took the stage disguised as Annie Hall, her ensemble typically independent and carefully orchestrated. Jane Fonda followed in the footsteps of Ingrid Bergman and wore the same dress two years in a row. Gary Busey expressed himself vividly a la *Halloween II* in an orange calico shirt, striped ribbon tie and black velvet suit. Raquel Welch closed out the decade in a cobalt-blue jumpsuit laden with sequins that only amplified Welch's endowments. No one was flaunting street fashion; each looked more Hollywood than the next. This was star style to savor.

At the fiftieth anniversary of the Academy Awards, Best Actress Diane Keaton received her Oscar for *Annie Hall* (1977) from Janet Gaynor, first Best Actress in 1928. In true Annie Hall fashion, under the menswear jacket she wore a striped full skirt and high heel pumps with anklet socks.

Asked to present the Irving G. Thalberg Award to Lawrence Weingarten in 1974, the iconoclastic Katharine Hepburn took command of the Academy podium dressed in gardening togs and clogs. Just before she went on, costume designers secured her rotting old Mao jacket with safety pins, which were then sprayed black to look like buttons. People backstage asked show producer Jack Haley, Jr., when she was going to get dressed. His response was "She *is* dressed!"

In 1977, Cicely Tyson presented the Irving G. Thalberg Memorial Award to producer Pandro S. Berman, wearing a tiered white lace gown with a floral choker.

The flowing medieval-inspired robe that Vanessa Redgrave wore in 1978 to accept her Supporting Actress Award for *Julia* (1977) was as controversial as were her political views in support of Palestinians. Outside the Dorothy Chandler Pavilion, protesters burned her in effigy.

In 1979, Jane Fonda took Best Actress honors for *Coming Home* (1978) dressed in a feathery print gown scattered with sparkling paillettes. The crowd felt Fonda's enthusiasm, especially since she had missed Best Actress honors the year before for her highly favored role in *Julia*.

# Actors and Oscars

"I'D LIKE TO THANK EVERYONE HERE tonight for looking so good." Thus spoke Jack Nicholson on Academy Awards night in 1998. He was quick to admit that he was wearing a Cerruti tuxedo, a Donna Karan shirt and a Gucci cummerbund. The ever-suave Nicholson caught himself being too chic, however, and quickly amended, "But fashion all comes from inside, anyway. Don't ya think?"

Until the 1970s nobody really thought about what men wore to the Oscars. The requisite tuxedo provided the appropriate background for the ladies in their dramatic finery. The biggest choice was whether to wear a boutonniere or a pocket square. The occasional deviation from the classic, such as Frank Sinatra's shiny sharkskin tux at the 1954 show, created no more than a blip in the annals of men's fashion. But when *Hair* was a smash on Broadway reinforcing the fact that it is the male peacock that gets all the attention, actors re-evaluated their feathers.

Men's fashion trends became apparent at the Awards when Sammy Davis, Jr., showed up in a braid-trimmed Nehru jacket in 1968 and Sonny Bono took the stand-up collar suit one step further and appeared in a silk damask version the same night. Sammy and Sonny had rebelled against the Academy's fashion rule maker, Edith Head, who had declared that male stylers eschew love beads and jeweled turtlenecks. Davis and Bono made the international newspapers the next day. What men wore to Hollywood's biggest night changed forever.

Robin Williams does a Marx Brothers' run after accepting the Best Supporting Actor Award for *Good Will Hunting* (1997). He credited his elongated tuxedo with band collared shirt as "Amish Armani."

"Don't I look like I can stand on top of a wedding cake?" Tom Selleck asked backstage before presenting the award for 1987 Best Animated Short Film along with co-presenter Mickey Mouse. His slicked-backed hair and wing-collared shirt were sharp competition for Mickey's birthday suit.

A Nehru-ed Sammy Davis, Jr., sang "Talk to the Animals" from *Dr. Doolittle* (1967) and then accepted its Best Song Award from flapper Barbra Streisand.

In the seventies, experimentation led to a rash of bad taste. It was an era when men learned what worked and what didn't. They took fashion risks, pushed trends to the limit and waited for the reactions.

By the time Dennis Hopper of *Easy Rider* (1969) fame came clad in a double-breasted velvet tuxedo topped with a ten-gallon hat (the Stetson was at least a dressy white one), the world's eyes were at least ready to view diversity, even if they couldn't accept it. By 1974, people were so attuned to men taking chances that there was only a minor furor over the notorious Robert Opal who streaked across the stage naked behind host David Niven. ("Ladies and gentleman, that was bound to happen. The only laugh that man would probably ever get is for stripping and showing off his shortcomings" commented a seemingly stunned Niven, a bit too glib for the event to be totally unplanned.) Audiences and Academy executives were probably somewhat grateful then in 1976 when Sylvester Stallone had unbuttoned his tuxedo shirt to expose a huge Sicilian medallion glistening on his bare chest—at least he was dressed. The crowd went wild.

For the majority, however, the tuxedo remained a boring staple throughout the century, not much different from the first one worn by Griswold Lorillard in Tuxedo Park, New York, in 1887. Almost a century later, variations on the tux on Oscar evening ranged from Mel Gibson's well-researched family tartan waistcoat to Stevie Wonder's rainbow hued sequined lapels to the Lou Gossett, Jr., black suede version to Daniel Day Lewis' Edwardian frock coat. Among celebrities who were willing to express themselves, many of the fashion statements were creative, memorable and, yes, in great taste. Those expressive types deserve to be celebrated. And they need offer no apologies for straying from tradition. ◆

Both Frank Sinatra and Donna Reed won Oscars in 1954 for their supporting roles in *From Here to Eternity* (1953), but his shiny silk tuxedo took best-dressed honors among the sea of matte-finish men's evening wear.

At Elton John's annual after-the-Oscars party, the host greets director Steven Spielberg who won Best Picture and Best Director Awards for *Schindler's List* (1993) in 1994. John wore formal military-inspired garb and the director opted for a classic tuxedo.

Cool Jack Nicholson and gorgeous Anjelica Huston—he made them quite the stylish team in the mid-seventies. Though he had opted for a Hawaiian shirt and tux at one ceremony, here he takes a conservative clothing approach, and adds the beret and shades for panache.

Nominated for his screenplay for *Do the Right Thing* (1989), Spike Lee sported a vibrantly hued Kente cloth from Kenya and a flat-brimmed felt hat accessorizing his Sabato Russo jacket. Always recording for posterity, Lee brought his hand-held camera.

In 1990, Best Actor winner Daniel Day-Lewis selected an Edwardian frock coat and velvet vest worn over an ivory silk shirt and pegged trousers, all designed by Britain's Katharine Hamnett. The star of *My Left Foot* (1989) added the floppy bow tie as a traditional touch.

General Colin Powell introduced clips from two war films nominated for Best Picture in 1999, *Saving Private Ryan* (1998) and *The Thin Red Line* (1998).

Robert Redford accepted the Best Director Award for *Ordinary People* (1980) in a classic tux and his otherwise casual flair.

In 1996 Quincy Jones put more thought into his trendy tuxedo than Sharon Stone would have the world believe she put into her outfit. She said she pulled the Gap turtleneck from the floor of her closet. The broad velvet lapels of his knee-length Giorgio Armani evening coat carried a ten-carat star-shaped diamond set in platinum from Harry Winston. Next to the star, Jones wore a rainbow ribbon, at the behest of Jesse Jackson, to protest that the Academy had nominated only one African-American.

In 1994 Winona Ryder spins to show off the delicate beaded fringe on this 1950s gown that borrowed its design from the 1920s.

In 1984 Steven Spielberg and his then-wife Amy Irving, Supporting Actress nominee, join Glenn Close. Both were wearing vintage lace: Close, a dress by Anne Ross, and Irving, an antique blouse teamed with a Ralph Lauren velvet skirt.

# Borrowing From the Past

NOT EVERY ACTRESS bound for the Academy Awards ceremony buys a new gown. Some prefer to buy old clothes—beautiful vintage designs that have stood the test of time. Lee Grant was one of the first—she found a gorgeous gown at a thrift store and wore it complete with flowers in her hair the night she took home an Oscar for Best Supporting Actress in *Shampoo* (1975). It was the same night that Lily Tomlin who was also nominated for Best Supporting Actress in *Nashville* (1975) opted for a Woolworth's tiara and a brocade gown that looked like it came from Grandma Tomlin's trunk. From then on the vintage looks became more and more sophisticated. Susan Sarandon wore an art deco gown in 1983 and that same year Jamie Lee Curtis walked the red carpet in a gown that once belonged to Marlene Dietrich.

Yet another approach to vintage dressing is wearing new dresses designed to look old. When Winona Ryder isn't wearing authentic 1920s styles, as she does on the opposite page, she elects gowns from the likes of Chanel or Badgley Mischka (shown on page 19) whose designers have borrowed heavily from history to create new couture pieces. Likewise, although she wore a new Ralph Lauren gown, Andie McDowell looked as if she had stepped out of the pages of F. Scott Fitzgerald when she added long pearls to Lauren's flapper-style dress and marcelled her hair. Annette Bening appeared in 1991 wearing a champagne-toned gown (shown on page 105) that Albert Wolsky had designed for the 1940s period-piece, *Bugsy* (1991). Both Sharon Stone and Mira Sorvino (pages 98 and 100 respectively) also turned to old Hollywood for glamour girl looks. But none could compare with Madonna the night she sang "Sooner or Later (I Always Get My Man)," the Best Song winner from *Dick Tracy* (1990), disguised as Marilyn Monroe (page 8). Though her Bob Mackie dress was new, it reflected an era when stars wanted the world to know they were stars. Borrowing gowns from the past has reassured them that they won't be confused. ◆

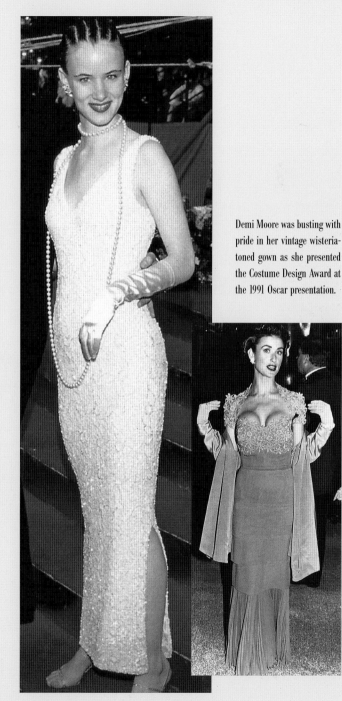

Demi Moore was busting with pride in her vintage wisteria-toned gown as she presented the Costume Design Award at the 1991 Oscar presentation.

Juliette Lewis liked cornrowed hair with the dress she purchased at a thrift shop for one hundred fifty dollars, a bargain amid the treasure trove of designer gowns at the Awards.

# Designer
## style

When the curtain went up at Los Angeles' Dorothy Chandler Pavilion in 1980, Oscar show producer Howard W. Koch had his fingers crossed that his "Elegant '80s" approach to the program would give it some sizzle. The most popular star scheduled to appear was Kermit the Frog singing "The Rainbow Connection," and the sexiest was Bo Derek, but Koch wasn't sure either could carry the show. Those marketing surveys from 1975 kept echoing in his brain: "…people actually care more about the clothes than who wins." To insure a high style quotient, he had hired Hollywood's biggest fashion gun to bring style and sex appeal to the show: Bob Mackie.

In 1980, Sally Field won the Best Actress Award for *Norma Rae* (1979). "She was trying not to look too serious," recalled her chosen designer, Bob Mackie. "She didn't want to look like she expected the Oscar." Her white wool suit with beaded chiffon blouse was a decided contrast to the luxe formal wear of the day.

Despite a paucity of glamorous stars on the stage that night, it was deemed a success. The next morning, fashion writers wrote about the gravity-defying support of Dolly Parton's fringed strapless gown, Meryl Streep's matronly Pauline Trigère evening suit, Ann Miller's blue Halston gown, and Bette Midler's understated antique kimono worn as a coat. Best Actress winner Sally Field's subdued white suit and beaded print blouse drew the most comment, since it was designed by Mackie and was totally different from his usual glitz-and-glamour outfits for Cher, Carol Burnett and Diana Ross. It was clear from the detailed reportage that the press was hungry for any information about celebrities and fashion. Extravagant style was about to become the symbol of the decade. The 1980s—the years of television's *Dallas* and *Dynasty*, Rodeo Drive and Giorgio Armani, breast implants and general excess—had begun.

Hollywood fashion was about as hot as it could be, both

When Cameron Diaz presented the 1997 Best Sound Award, she looked somewhat casual in a two-piece Chloe ensemble designed by Stella McCartney, daughter of Beatle Paul McCartney. She's shown here with actor Matt Dillon.

for the public and the celebrities. Rodeo Drive was the busiest shopping street in the world. Movie stars couldn't get enough Armani, Versace, Giorgio (the glitzy store *and* its powerful perfume), and Nolan Miller (whose big-shouldered designs for Joan Collins and Linda Evans were showcased on

TV's *Dynasty* every Wednesday night). Saks Fifth Avenue introduced Christian Lacroix's Parisian couture collection at Twentieth Century Fox studios, drawing more than six hundred Hollywood types to a gala party.

On the Academy Awards stage, stars attempted to make fashion an interesting subtext to a boring show. Cher, for one, always succeeded. Although her ensembles were not consistently well-received by the press, her fans were in fashion heaven every time she walked on the stage. In 1986 to present the Best Supporting Actor Award, she showed up in a black Mackie showgirl outfit that caused viewers to barely notice poor Don Ameche, who won the Award. The headdress itself was two-feet tall from the top of her forehead to the tip of its plumes. She told the audience "As you can see, I did receive my Academy booklet on how to dress like a serious actress." That costume was so shockingly sexual that years later, sponsor Coca-Cola requested the right to approve Cher's gown. Cher had achieved her goal. As *Glamour* magazine said in 1988, Cher "single-handedly makes the Oscars worth watching."

Many stars appreciated her guts and tried to make fashion statements too. Some designed their own clothes: Angelica Huston showed up in a one-shouldered emerald green gown she created in 1986 to accept her Best Supporting Actress Award for *Prizzi's Honor* (1985). Demi Moore, as a presenter for the 1988 awards, designed a bustier cum black-and-gold eighteenth century-inspired skirt (homage to the Best Picture of the day *Dangerous Liaisons*) that was cut away in front to expose a pair of twentieth century-inspired black spandex bike shorts. Kim Basinger took credit away from her onetime Svengali, the Artist Formerly Known As Prince, when she appeared in a one-shouldered fizzle, a white satin suit that might have been pretty if it had two sleeves. "Prince didn't help me on this one," she boasted. "It's a Kim Basinger original." Only Geena Davis and Cher, whose lanky bodies looked great in anything that hung on them, were successful—

Jodie Foster chose her best look in 1995 when as Best Actress nominee for *Nell* (1994) she wore an Armani gown encrusted with ivory beads that created an antique essence.

though criticized—when they took design into their own hands. "Thank God, no designer is to blame," was all *Women's Wear Daily*, the catty fashion trade paper, could say about actresses' noble loving-hands-at-home attempts to bring glamour back to Hollywood. It was clear: movie stars needed fashion designers. In the bygone days, actors and actresses had the luxury of studio designers at their beck and call. But studios no longer had staff designers, so stars turned to fashion designers.

Italian fashion design star Giorgio Armani had always loved Hollywood and the movies. So when Diane Keaton chose one of his slouchy men's jackets to wear as part of her Annie Hall getup for the Academy Awards in 1978, the show was already in his blood. He had his first working taste of Hollywood in 1980 when he created the costumes for the movie *American Gigolo (1980)*, giving Richard Gere's character a designer wardrobe so notable that an entire scene was devoted to laying out his clothes in preparation for a trip. The next year Armani racked up sales of ninety million dollars and the savvy designer saw the importance of courting Hollywood. And so did his competition.

A new job quickly emerged in Beverly Hills: socially and professionally connected women were hired to be liaisons between the fashion designers and the film and television industry. A major goal was to get Hollywood stars zipped into designer clothing on Oscar night. It was a form of product placement: just as Reese's Pieces got a huge sales boost after they were placed in the film *E.T. (1982)*, designer labels would become more desirable, the fashion moguls reasoned, if their clothes were seen on famous people. It was worth it to

When she presented the Costume Design Award in 1995, Sharon Stone selected a satin Vera Wang gown that could have doubled as a wedding gown. Underneath the jacket was a strapless beaded bodice.

Red-haired Shirley MacLaine sparkled as she claimed the Best Actress Award for *Terms of Endearment* (1983) wearing a blush-colored knee-length dress and cardigan by Fabrice.

In 1996, landmarks in style appeared on the red carpet. Gwyneth Paltrow (top left), who had yet to reach superstardom, and her then-beau Best Supporting Actor nominee Brad Pitt were more casual than the Oscar crowd had ever seen. His shirt was open and she stared pale faced into cameras with her surfer-girl hair and shapeless Calvin Klein slip dress. At the opposite extreme, but still a trendsetter, the Best Supporting Actress was fifties glamour girl Mira Sorvino (shown at left on the arm of Quentin Tarantino) in a silver Armani and blond hair styled a la Lana Turner. Also trendsetting was the gown worn by Documentary Award presenter Elisabeth Shue. The simple twist at the shoulder and uplifting corset bodice created the neckline of the nineties, a contrast to the unconstructed slip dress. "I need a bra," she admitted. Designed by Felicia Farrar, Shue's ivory satin dress had a train.

give a celebrity a ten-thousand-dollar gown if she would wear it on the televised show. While it may seem like a simple task, it wasn't easy to achieve. It took a full-time person to network and follow through. Armani hired Wanda McDaniel in 1988, the former society editor of a Los Angeles daily newspaper and the wife of film mogul Al Ruddy, to start making Hollywood connections.

One of her first accomplishments was to have Michelle Pfeiffer glide onto the 1989 stage swathed in his navy blue crepe suit with jeweled buttons. But it was in 1990, when a stunning Jodie Foster, who had never been known for her fashion finesse, appeared at the Oscars in a black Armani jacket and knee-length slim skirt, that the public took notice of the designer's name. How could they not, since the same year Julia Roberts went braless under one of his taupe gowns, Jessica Tandy teamed his beaded midnight blue jacket and skirt, and Michelle Pfeiffer again slinked into the ceremony in Armani, this time an indigo sheath. With that many women (and even more men) wearing his clothes, it only made sense that by 1991, he was seated in the audience at the Awards, cheering his favorite stars in his favorite gowns.

There were so many Armani-clad winners, losers and presenters, men and women alike, that in 1991 *Women's Wear Daily* devoted a whole page to the phenomenon. "The Armani Awards," the headline read. Thus began the biggest fashion competition in the world. Who would get Streisand? Who would get Sharon Stone? Liaisons for Calvin Klein, Gianni Versace, Krizia, Cerruti, Ralph Lauren, Prada and the like spent their time trying to get into agents' offices to negotiate the biggest deals of their careers. Nominees and presenters were suddenly bombarded with offers of free clothes or clothes on loan. Best Actress contenders and

Obviously pleasing her husband Tom Cruise, Nicole Kidman appeared in 1996 to present the Film Editing Award wearing a simple gown by Prada, the Italian house that had never made evening wear before Uma Thurman wore the label in 1995.

especially the front runner, had too many gowns from which to choose. At one point, Best Actress nominee Diane Keaton told the *Los Angeles Times*, "Nobody's called me [to offer free gowns]. Now we know for sure they didn't expect me." Likewise, when he was nominated for Best Actor, Jim Carrey's then-wife Lauren Holly was offered fifty-six different gowns for free, all she had to do was wear one and name the designer if asked.

As designers were forging their strategies, the Academy got the fashion bug too. To help make certain that any star could look high-fashion even if he or she didn't know how, the Academy asked Fred Hayman to serve as the official fashion consultant for the 1989 ceremonies. The first long-term replacement for Edith Head (who had died in 1981), Hayman had built his reputation as the creative mind behind Giorgio, the legendary boutique on Rodeo Drive immortalized by Judith Krantz' novel *Scruples*. (His store was so renowned, in fact, that it sold an eponymous perfume that became the best-selling fragrance in the world.) Often credited with master-minding the success of Rodeo Drive, Hayman established the goal to bring Hollywood glamour back to the Academy Awards. Initially he didn't intend to make it the most spec-tacular fashion show in the world, but that's exactly what happened.

Hayman's first step was to generate anticipation for the fashions that would be seen at the ceremony. Hayman con-ceived the pre-Awards fashion show, held several weeks before the ballots were counted. His commentary projected fashion trends for Oscar night while models paraded the runway and television news cameras recorded every gown. Newscasts all over the world spread the word that, to honor Awards night, Hollywood would soon be going all out for glamour.

Sigourney Weaver chose this exquisite Christian Lacroix gown for a reason beyond its beauty, she admitted in 1995. "I just wanted to be able to say 'Sweetie, Darling, it's Lacroix!'"

In 1995, Jennifer Tilley and supermodel Vendela selected the same Isaac Mizrahi gown in different colors. The dark-haired Tilley made a point not to be photographed anywhere near the svelte blonde. Despite insecurities about her figure, in the final analysis, it was Tilley who gave the sequinned dress its curvaceous movie-star panache.

With a billion people tuned in to see what their favorite stars were wearing, dressing for the occasion became so important that some perfectionistic celebrities started planning months before they knew they were attending the event—just in case. Those who were too busy to plan their attire hired stylists to coordinate gowns, jewels, shoes and other accessories. When she was nominated for Best Supporting Actress for *Sense and Sensibility* (1995), Kate Winslet was deep into filming *Kenneth Branagh's Hamlet*. (1996). She handed over the responsibility of her Oscar night garb to London-based stylist Marion Hume, who immediately started rejecting designers left and right, until she hit upon the hometown label of Vivienne Westwood, queen of romanticism in cloth. In the hands of Westwood's corsetiere, a body that might have looked zaftig in Calvin Klein, looked ready for a Victorian portraitist, taller and leaner than she had ever looked. Hume ordered handmade hot pink shoes to match the ensemble from another local, Jimmy Choo, and even sourced an Irish lace handkerchief, in case Winslet got teary. Winslet didn't win, but Hume's taste had established her as a serious star, and in what seemed like no time, she was up for Best Actress in *Titanic* (1997).

Jessica Tilley's stylist didn't help quite as much, making her trek to Isaac Mizrahi's New York design quarters to work alone with the designer. Mizrahi zipped her into a blue-black sequinned gown ("It reminded me of Jessica Rabbit," Tilley recalls) and only after she decided to take it, did he mention that supermodel Vendela was wearing the same dress in raspberry. Rather than be compared to the cover girl—or worse yet, photographed alongside her—"I put my sister on Vendela watch." Her sister would run ahead of her, make sure the coast was clear (no Vendela in sight), and beckon Tilley to proceed along the red carpet. A sharper stylist would have foreseen the problem and avoided it, but Tilley's sister wouldn't have had half as much fun.

Designer Alexander McQueen summed up the stylist situation in an interview with *Vogue* magazine, "I don't think that there are any real style icons in Hollywood—not like in the Monroe days. Actresses are so overdone by their stylists and the media, it is difficult to actually see their own personal style." Glenn Close voiced concerns that stars had given up their Hollywood-given right to individuality. "If you wear Armani, chances are no one will write anything negative about your dress," she observed. "But you have to learn to be immune to the criticism and just wear what you like."

Many stars have had problems making final dress decisions until a day or two before the Awards. Julia Roberts and Los Angeles-based designer Richard

To present the 1991 Academy Award for Art Direction, Annette Bening wore an actual costume from *Bugsy* the movie she was in the process of filming with Warren Beatty, her leading man and soon-to-be husband. According to costume designer, Albert Wolsky, she went directly from the set in the 1940s style gown and only changed her hairstyle to look more current.

Tyler put their heads together just a few days before the 1990 Awards were to be given out. The Best Supporting Actress nominee was actually being sewn into the gown in the limousine, as they proceeded to the Shrine Auditorium. Another last minute dresser, Sharon Stone told the world that she found the charcoal Gap turtleneck she wore to the 1996 awards on the floor of her closet. That she paired it with what she called "old clothing" (a Valentino trumpet skirt and full length black silk velvet Giorgio Armani coat) was just a stroke of luck, or so she'd like her public to believe. Ditto for the year she "borrowed" her husband's white shirt that she teamed with a lavender Vera Wang skirt for another offhand Oscar look. Whether these outfits were indeed last-minute decisions or, perhaps, strategically planned "last-minute" looks, only she and her favorite fashion stylist can know for sure. Teaming daywear with evening looks suddenly became a trend that the boldest fashion iconoclasts chanced. Clare Danes turned to Narciso Rodriguez (the designer who gained fame when he designed the gown Carolyn Bessette wore to wed John Kennedy) for a simple short-sleeved cashmere sweater atop a sleek silk skirt and then added a twenty-three-thousand-dollar blue topaz and diamond necklace. A look back at history shows that it wasn't Stone or Danes who first took the casual approach, however. Rather it was Katharine Hepburn, who in 1974 approached the podium to present the Irving Thalberg Award wearing her coolie-styled gardening togs. She even called attention to her clothes in her speech, referring to them, with tongue in cheek, as "her lovelies."

Hepburn, however, did not donate those gardening togs to a star-studded Christie's auction benefiting American Federation for AIDS Research (AmFAR). Danes did donate

Nominated for 1998 Best Actress for her role in *Elizabeth* (1998), Cate Blanchett liked the back appeal of her John Galliano gown. "I feel like I'm having a fashion orgasm," she said of the knitted dress whose back was embroidered with flowers and a hummingbird at the Parisian atelier of Francois Lesage. The gown sold for fifteen thousand dollars at Christie's AmFAR auction.

In 1987, Best Actress nominees Kathleen Turner and Sigourney Weaver shared a pre-show moment. Weaver, in a strapless Geoffrey Beene gown, wore dramatic earrings that Turner coveted, "Lord, I want those earrings," she declared. "They're a performance in themselves."

Jessica Tandy won the 1989 Best Actress Award for *Driving Miss Daisy* (1989) wearing navy-blue beaded jacket by Giorgio Armani. New York Post columnist Cindy Adams hailed the victor: "Forget the seventeen-year-old tawny-haired twinkies. Last night the Big Star was Jessica Tandy."

Liv Tyler introduced the nominated song "I Don't Want to Miss a Thing" from *Armageddon* (1998) in a platinum-toned strapless dress designed by New York designer Pamela Dennis.

addition, Christie's sold fifteen thousand copies of the auction catalog, a picture book entitled *Unforgettable Fashion of the Oscars.*

Another donation came from Uma Thurman: the beaded lavender gown designed for the night she was nominated for Best Supporting Actress in *Pulp Fiction* (1994). She didn't win that night, but her dress helped change the face of Oscar fashion. At the opposite end of the spectrum from the body-hugging, shimmering gowns that had been popular ever since Ann-Margret wore one in 1962, Thurman's was derived from a simple daytime shift designed by Miuccia Prada. Prada had sent designs to Los Angeles for Thurman's selection, but none were evening gowns. Viewing the sketches with Los Angeles-based costume designer, Barbara Tfank, who had served as liaison between Prada and the star, Thurman rejected the entire collection just ten days before the ceremony. Knowing that Prada was anxious to have one of its gowns appear on the show and that the clothes suited

her blue sweater and skirt. The 1999 auction, conceived by actress Natasha Richardson, was comprised of more than fifty gowns worn to the Oscar ceremonies and raised eight hundred thousand dollars for the charity. Although Danes' dress drew three thousand dollars, that sizable amount seemed minor compared to the one hundred seventy thousand dollars Liz Taylor's lavender blue Edith Head drew. Buyers ranged from individuals eager to own them to clothing manufacturers and retailers with designs on selling copies of the gown. In

Many women have worn menswear looks to the Oscars, but none with as much aplomb as the tuxedoed Whoopi Goldberg, the Oscar ceremony host in 1994. In years past, there have been several attempts to give men's evening attire a curvier form: Diana Ross, in a silver tux with a rhinestone vest by Bob Mackie, 1973; Ellen Burstyn, in a black tux with a ruffled blue shirt, 1977; Ellen DeGeneres and Celine Dion, both in white tuxes (DeGeneres wore hers with a black shirt and Dion's was backwards, a la Christian Dior), 1999.

Busy filming a new movie in London when she was named a nominee for Best Supporting Actress in *Sense and Sensibility* (1995), Kate Winslet had very little to do with the selection of this pink gown by Vivienne Westwood, but it remains one of her most flattering images.

Wearing a cashmere sweater and silk charmeuse skirt by Narciso Rodriguez for Cerruti, newcomer Clare Danes presented the Original Song Production number from *That Thing You Do* (1996).

Thurman's body, Tfank saved the day. She suggested that one of the lean daytime looks could be adapted to suit the very dressy needs of Academy Awards night. On the spot Tfank called in costume designer John David Ridge, who had been design director at Halston for several years, and together they shaped two gowns: a short-sleeved yellow one and the lavender one Thurman selected. Tfank and Ridge maintained the simplicity of Prada's sleeveless, scoop-neck day dress, added princess seaming to allow the dress to glide over Thurman's silhouette, extended the length to the floor and added a beaded chiffon overlay. Prada provided the beads that were artfully strewn on the chiffon to the hem. As Ridge tells the story, "I shopped for the fabric at Eastern Silk Co. in Los Angeles, it was designed and sewn in Los Angeles, and I stitched in the Prada label, and the 'Made in Italy' tag." The day of the Awards, Thurman came in for her last fitting and to decide which gown she would wear, Prada had also sent a gown that was actually designed and constructed in its Italian workrooms, but Thurman selected the lavender, made-in-L.A. gown. She wore a pale beaded chiffon stole over the dress and carried a lavender satin evening bag. The pivotal change of color and shape in Thurman's gown influenced Academy Award fashions for the rest of the century. And the gown raised eight thousand dollars at auction.

The next year, at the 1996 presentation, show producer Quincy Jones, himself a fashion devotee, hired noted photographer and video director, Matthew Rolston to stage a runway fashion extravaganza to showcase the work of the Costume Design Award nominees. Using the current fashion models of the day—Claudia Schiffer, Naomi Campbell, Niki Taylor, Bridget Hall and Tyra Banks—Rolston brought all the excitement of European fashion shows to the Oscar stage. A highlight of the evening's program, the format surprisingly was not used again.

Fashion and Oscar had converged completely. Any star who hoped to be a Big Star understood the power of her

Goldie Hawn selected a pistachio-toned Versace gown when she and her long-time companion Kurt Russell presented the 1995 Best Film Editing Award. Her bib necklace contained one hundred twenty carats of diamonds.

In 1995, Holly Hunter wore the sheer Vera Wang style that became a classic look at the Oscars. She presented Tom Hanks with his Best Actor Award for *Forrest Gump* (1994).

perceived style. She knew she could create her image and manipulate her audience with her star style. Gwyneth Paltrow became the clear example. Though she attended the Awards with a surfer-girl casualness in a shapeless Calvin Klein gown when she attended as the date of nominee Brad Pitt in 1996, she took another approach when she was nominated for Best Actress. Paltrow elected to surprise the Academy Award viewers in 1999 by not wearing a sexy Klein. Or a sophisticated Armani. Or a Narciso Rodriguez, the designer of that hour. Instead she chose to look, as she put it, "sweet." In sugarplum pink, she strode to the stage to accept her Best Actress Award for *Shakespeare in Love* (1998), sweet as apple pie in a gown by America's classic Ralph Lauren. Looking quite like the innocent ingenue in a gown too big for her seemingly yet-to-form bosoms, the only classic indication of her star power was at her neck: a band of rock candy, all one hundred sixty thousand dollars worth. How sweet she was.

So closed the twentieth century of Academy Awards nights. It will always be remembered as a century of fashion that evolved as the movie stars evolved. A century of glamour. At least where the Oscar is concerned.

Best Supporting Actress nominee Uma Thurman startled fashion experts in 1995 by wearing a Prada gown. "I didn't know Prada made evening dresses," said Sigourney Weaver. "They don't," retorted Thurman. "They just made this one."

# Geena Davis

GEENA DAVIS SAYS SHE REMEMBERS being a child dreaming of becoming a famous star. Talk about dreams coming true. In the process she became a symbol of fashion at the Oscar show, upping the evening's glamour quotient each time she appeared. Some critics would say that the former model tested the limits of her style a few times on the Oscar stage, but her successes were so numerous that it's difficult to find fault when she dares to be different. Like Cher, Davis has become a fashion legend at the Academy Awards, a woman whose gown is always worthy of comment… and usually of praise.

Her first appearance, when she accepted her Best Supporting Actress Award for *Accidental Tourist* (1988), was in an ice-blue satin gown designed by Hollywood's Bill Hargate. A storybook dress complete with a princess's flounce on its backside, the gown was the perfect introduction for a fledgling star, a statement in romantic cool. The following year, when Davis presented the Best Supporting Actor Award, another collaboration with Hargate didn't disappoint. All seventy-two inches of her body were wrapped in shirred red silk that dropped

1993                1989

off her shoulders exposing as much skin as the censors would allow. Attending with then-husband Jeff Goldblum, who had starred with her in *The Fly* (1986), she was every inch a star. The dress was a winner.

At the Awards show in 1992, when Davis was in line for Best Actress for *Thelma and Louise* (1991), designers Ruth Myers and Hargate created the star's first loser. In a burst of creativity, the Hollywood designers shaped a short white satin gown with a long ruffled train. Davis donned black silk stockings to match the black spaghetti straps, ribbons and lace insets in the train; her most unfortunate look was born. The press likened her image to everything from a hookah-smoking caterpillar and Big Bird in dust ruffles to a drunken can-can girl. Even the harshest critics had to admit, however, that the dress simply suffered from bad design—Davis carried it off with her typical dimpled charm. Her smiling visage was in newspapers and magazines all over the world the next morning.

By 1993 she had a new husband, director Renny Harlin, and a new look at the Oscars. With her hair worn long a la Lauren Bacall, her image was befitting her role to introduce the ceremony's special film-clip segment called "A Tribute to Women."

Appearing in what was perhaps one of the most copied necklines of the nineties, Davis drew major applause when she stepped to the microphone in Hargate's black velvet column with a deep, curving decolletage. Harlin's influence showed up again the following year when Davis's hair was long and her sparkling gown was white. Both looks were sophisticated, but lacked the fanciful drama of her earliest Oscar looks. It was not until the couple split in 1997 that Davis found her own style again.

1990 - 1998

To present a clip from one of the nominees for the 1997 Best Picture, Davis selected a pale peach Halston floor-length tube worn with a matching fox-trimmed shrug. With that one great dress she regained her stature as one of the most fashionable women at the Oscars. She was, in fact, so established that the Academy selected her to host its first official pre-show, which included a tribute to fashion through the years at the Oscars. In a startling example of old Hollywood meeting new media, Davis posed for a number of fashion photographs prior to the event and those shots were distributed on the Internet to promote her show.

Later that night, on the Oscar stage, Davis, as a presenter, changed from the corseted structure of the pink Bradley Bayou gown she had worn on the pre-show into the graceful ease of a rhinestone-studded silk gown by the former Halston designer, Randolph Duke, a gown obviously shaped precisely to suit her perfect body.

If fashion legends are born in Hollywood, certainly Geena Davis qualifies. Hers is a look that she controls, independent of studios and stylists. While her contemporaries have been showered with free wardrobes from powerful designers the world over, Davis works with the artists who suit her aesthetic sense and who honor her body and sense of style over their own design. ◆

1999

# Index

Photographs on preceding pages:
Goldie Hawn, Diane Keaton
 and Bette Midler, 1997
Sophia Loren, 1999
Jennifer Lopez, 1999
Uma Thurman, 1999
Madonna, 1997
Steve Martin, Goldie Hawn
 and Kurt Russell, 1999
Hank Azaria and Helen Hunt, 1998
Eddie Fisher and Elizabeth Taylor, 1961
Phil Bronstein and Sharon Stone, 1998
Bette Midler, 1992
Stevie Wonder, 1985
Shirley MacLaine, 1959
Courtney Love, 1997

# BIBLIOGRAPHY

Regine and Peter Engelmeier (editors), *Fashion and Film*, Prestel Berglag, Munich, 1990.

Patty Fox, *Star Style: Hollywood Legends as Fashion Icons*, Angel City Press, Santa Monica, 1995.

Leslie Halliwell, *Halliwell's Film Guide*, Charles Scribner's Sons, New York, 1982.

Edith Head and Paddy Calistro, *Edith Head's Hollywood*, E.P. Dutton, New York, 1983.

Anthony Holden, *Behind the Oscar: The Secret History of the Academy Awards*, Simon & Schuster, New York, 1993.

Hedda Hopper and James Brough, *The Whole Truth and Nothing But*, Doubleday & Co., New York, 1963.

Emanuel Levy, *And the Winner is… The History and Politics of the Oscar Awards*, Ungar Publishing Company, New York, 1987.

Robert Osborne, *60 Years of the Oscar: The Official History of the Academy Awards*, Abbeville Press, New York, 1989.

Mason Wiley and Damien Bona, *Inside Oscar: The Unofficial History of the Academy Awards*, Ballantine Books, New York, 1993.

# PHOTO CREDITS

The author is grateful to the following individuals and institutions for their photographic contributions to *Star Style at the Academy Awards*. Their photographs appear on pages specified here:

**Academy of Motion Pictures Arts and Sciences Center for Motion Picture Study Margaret Herrick Library**: 3 right, 8, 10, 28, 31, 34 right, 37 left, 44, 58, 65, 66, 67, 73, 74, 76, 77, 79, 81, 90, 92, 93, 115, 125 left, 126, 128 left. **Jerry Anderson**: 5 left, 106, 119 left, 122 left, 123 right. **Archive Photos**: 11 (Saga), 12, 19 (Darlene Hammond), 30 (American Stock), 37 right, 48, 50 right, 51, 59 (Popperfoto), 62, 86 (Max Miller/Fotos International), 87, 88 (Max Miller/Fotos International), 89 right (Saga), 93 (John McCoy/L.A. Daily News/Saga), 97 (L.A. Daily News/Saga), 98 (L.A. Daily News/Saga), 103 (Alison Waggner/Fotos International), 104 (L.A. Daily News/Saga), 105 (Saga), 112 and 113 (Darlene Hammond), 116, 117 right (Fotos/ International), 118 left (Darlene Hammond), 123 left, 124 left (Saga), 125 right (Reuters/Fred Prouser). **Bison Archives/ Marc Wanamaker**: 22 through 27, 32, 33, 35, 38, 40, 42 right, 46, 50 left, 56, 59, 60 right, 72, 99. **Tyson Board**: 3 left, 5 right, 15 left, 18, 60 left, 96, 100 through 102, 111, 118 right, 122 right. **Sean Brady**: 91 right, 114. **Celebrity Photo Agency**: 61 top, 63. **Robert Cohn collection**: 9. **Michael Jacobs**: 14 left, 89 left, 107, 124 right. **Jay Kelbley**: 4 right, 36 right, 110. **Photofest**: 1, 2 left, 6, 12 inset, 16, 20, 34 left, 36 left, 41, 42 left, 43 (Walt Davis), 47, 52 through 54, 61 bottom, 64, 68, 70, 71, 75, 78, 80, 83, 91 left, 94, 108, 117 left. **Regional History Center, Special Collections, University of Southern California Library**: 57. **Mike Resar**: 2 right, 4 left, 7 right, 85, 90 left, 109, 119 right, 120 and 121. **Greg Schreiner**: 49. **Lou Valentino**: 55. **Tom Zimmerman**: 14 right, 15 right, 84.

Don Adams, Eastman Kodak Entertainment Imaging director, gets a kiss from Gwyneth Paltrow, 1999.

Much of the color imagery in this book has been supplied by Resar Entertainment, which formed the Academy Awards digital photography team. With Kodak friends and associates, the team includes: back row: Drena Rogers, Mike Resar, Tim Resar, Sean Brady, Kathy Resar, Nancy Tate, Don Adams, Steve Adams, Steve Gonnella, Serina Mayer, Tyson Board, Karla Pierce; front row: Bob Cosway, Jay Resar, Fred Barajas. Not shown: Jerry Anderson and Jay Kelbley, Larry Rogers, Dan Bourgault and Kyle Leonhardt.

# KINGDOM CLASSIFICATION

## REDWOODS, HEMLOCKS & OTHER
# CONE-BEARING PLANTS

By Steve Parker

*First published in the United States in 2009 by*
Compass Point Books
151 Good Counsel Drive
P.O. Box 669
Mankato, MN 56002-0669

KINGDOM CLASSIFICATION—CONE-BEARING PLANTS
was produced by

**David West Children's Books**
7 Princeton Court
55 Felsham Road
London SW15 1AZ

*Designer:* Rob Shone
*Editors:* Gail Bushnell, Anthony Wacholtz
*Page Production:* Bobbie Nuytten

*Creative Director:* Joe Ewest
*Art Director:* LuAnn Ascheman-Adams
*Editorial Director:* Nick Healy
*Managing Editor:* Catherine Neitge

Library of Congress Cataloging-in-Publication Data
Parker, Steve, 1952–
  Redwoods, hemlocks & other cone-bearing plants / by Steve Parker.
    p. cm.—(Kingdom classifications)
  Includes index.
  ISBN 978-0-7565-4221-4 (library binding)
  1. Conifers—Juvenile literature.
I. Title. II. Title: Redwoods, hemlocks and other cone-bearing plants. III. Series: Parker, Steve, 1952– Kingdom classifications.
  QK494.P37 2010
  585—dc22          2009012608

Visit Compass Point Books on the Internet at
*www.compasspointbooks.com*
or e-mail your request to
*custserv@compasspointbooks.com*

*Front cover: Blue Spruce*
*Opposite: Lebanon Cedar*

# REDWOODS, HEMLOCKS & OTHER
# CONE-BEARING PLANTS

*Steve Parker*

Compass Point Books ✦ Minneapolis, Minnesota

# CONTENTS

# INTRODUCTION

Trees such as pines, firs, cedars, cypresses, spruces, redwoods, larches, and yews are all conifers. Most are evergreen—they keep some of their leaves all year round, rather than shedding them in the fall, as deciduous trees do. The leaves of many conifers are needle-shaped or scalelike. Rather than producing seeds from flowers or blossoms, conifers get their name from the woody structures called cones where their seeds develop.

Conifers are important—both in nature and to humans. They are found in many habitats, especially in extreme conditions where the climate is cold and snowy, dry, or swampy. They are found along cliffs, in valleys, and on mountains. Conifer trees provide shelter, food, and homes to many species of animals. They also supply us with wood for making furniture, houses, fences, paper, and many other products.

## GREEN ALL YEAR

*Most conifers have at least some leaves all year round. Small amounts of leaves usually fall off at regular intervals. There are also times in spring or fall when more leaves grow and the tree looks fuller.*

# WHAT ARE CONIFERS?

Conifers belong to the plant division known as Pinophyta or Coniferae. Their main feature is their cones, in which they make seeds.

## COMMON CONES

*The cones of the limber pine in western North America have a common conical shape and clustered woody parts known as scales.*

## CONES AND SEEDS

There are more than 630 species of conifers growing around the world. Most conifers are trees or shrubs. Their seeds are usually produced inside brown, wooden structures known as cones. These include the familiar pine and fir cones. However, a few conifers, such as yews and junipers, produce their seeds inside softer, more colorful structures that look like berries.

## FLOWERS AND BLOSSOMS

*Flowering plants make their seeds in flowers or blossoms, not in cones. Flowers, such as the poppy (above), have soft petals and are often very colorful.*

## FOLIAGE

*Conifer leaves are usually narrow, stiff, tough, and sharp-edged. Examples of conifers are the Chile pine (above), Englemann spruce (left), and Atlantic white cypress (right).*

## SHAPES

*Conifers have a variety of shapes. Some are wide and spreading, like the Lebanon cedar (right). Others are tall and come to a pointed tip, such as the Brewer's spruce (below). The stone pine (far right), with its crown of leaves, looks like an umbrella.*

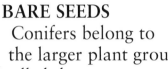

## BARE SEEDS

Conifers belong to the larger plant group called the gymnosperms, which means "naked seeds." The seeds are formed inside the cone, but they are not covered or enclosed. In the other group of seed-producing plants—the angiosperms (flowering plants)—the seeds are usually covered or enclosed in a fruit.

## CONIFER CELEBRATION

Conifers provide greenery during the winter and are used in many kinds of celebrations and festivals around the world. One example is a Christmas tree, which is decorated with lights, ornaments, and presents. The species of trees used vary according to the region, but they are usually firs—such as the silver or balsam fir—or spruces, such as the Norway spruce.

*A Christmas tree is a cheerful sight during the winter.*

### STICKY RESIN

*Many conifers have sticky sap that oozes from a cut. This helps seal the "wound" and prevent disease.*

9

# PREHISTORIC CONIFERS

**M**any of the broad-leaved trees with flowers that exist today appeared less than 50 million years ago. Before that, conifers were more common.

## ANCIENT FORESTS

*The Chile pine* Araucaria araucana *has a long history. Forests of Chile pines growing today (above) resemble those from the time of the dinosaurs.*

## PETRIFIED FORESTS

*Conifer trunks, branches, cones, and entire forests from millions of years ago have been preserved. Some scientists believe that nearby volcanoes erupted and showered the areas with hot ash. The ash killed and preserved the trees as they turned into rock, forming "petrified forests."*

## THE FIRST TREES

Conifers were among the first large trees to grow on land. Their origins go back to the Carboniferous period, about 300 million years ago, when prehistoric amphibians were crawling out of the swamps and becoming the first reptiles. Other ancient trees and treelike plants included ginkgos and cycads. Like conifers, they are in the gymnosperm group. They formed vast forests where dinosaurs roamed and fed.

## CONIFER FOSSILS

*We know about prehistoric life from fossils—the remains and impressions of plants and animals that have been preserved in the rocks and turned to stone. Examples of conifer fossils include a fossilized redwood stump (left) in Colorado and fossil cones of an araucaria pine (above).*

## PERFECTLY PRESERVED

Wood, cones, and leaves from ancient conifers have been fossilized—and so has their sticky resin. Over millions of years, it has hardened into yellow amber. Insects and other small animals became trapped and perfectly preserved in the resin.

*Lumps of amber contain insects, spiders, and even small frogs and mice, with every detail still visible.*

## DINOSAUR FOOD

*Plant-eating dinosaurs from about 70 million years ago include the hadrosaurs, such as Edmontosaurus (below). These duck-billed dinosaurs had rows of hundreds of flat, ridged teeth used to grind tough conifer and cycad leaves into a soft pulp.*

## CONIFER COUSINS

There are about 300 living species of cycads. Their fossilized leaves have been found with the bones of dinosaurs and other ancient animals. Today there is only one type of ginkgo, called the ginkgo or maidenhair tree. But 100 million years ago, there were many others.

### CYCADS

*Prehistoric cycads and cycadeoids included Williamsonia, Cycadites, and Zamites (left). They were similar to modern species (above right).*

11

# HOW CONIFERS GROW

Like most other plants, conifers grow from seeds. Within a seed is a tiny plant, the embryo, as well as food for its first weeks of growth.

***SEEDLINGS***
*Conifer seeds start to form seedlings when the weather is warm and there is moisture in the air.*

## GROWTH RINGS

The main stem of a conifer is called the trunk. If you cut through the trunk, you will find alternating light and dark rings. A light ring forms when the tree grows quickly in the spring. A dark ring represents a time of slower growth in late summer. Each light-and-dark ring combination represents one year of growth. Wider rings show years of extra growth in good conditions.

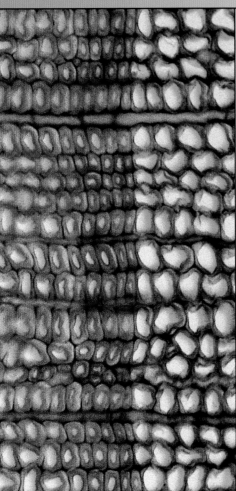

### *MICRO-TUBES*

*A microscope view (left) shows a cross-section of the phloem tubes in spring (right side) and summer (left side).*

## INSIDE THE TRUNK

Under the protective outer bark of a conifer tree is the inner bark, called phloem (bast). It has thousands of microscopic tubes that carry nutrient-rich sap to all parts of the tree. Beneath the phloem is the xylem (sapwood). It also has micro-tubes, which take water and soil minerals from the roots up to the leaves. Between these two layers is the thin cambium layer, in which new phloem and xylem are made. The heartwood is made of dead sapwood.

Outer bark

Growth rings

Phloem (inner bark)

Cambium

Heartwood    Sapwood    Xylem

12

Crown

Leader

## BUDS, SHOOTS, AND LEAVES

The upper leafy part of the tree, called the crown, produces side buds that grow into longer shoots. The crown then forms twigs, branches, and cones. The main central shoot, called the leader, continues straight upward.

## STRINGY BARK

The bark differs in various conifers. In redwoods it is soft and stringy and can be up to 12 inches (30 centimeters) thick.

## UPPER BARK

Younger bark, which is higher in the tree, is less flaky, worn, and scarred from age, weather, and wood-boring insects and other creatures.

## ROOTS

Roots of conifers grow into the soil, but they usually don't divide as much as the roots of broad-leaved trees. They hold the tree in the soil, take in water and nutrients, and keep it from falling over in high winds. Scotch pine roots (below) were exposed after a flood.

Missing branches

Cones

## CONES

In most conifers, the cones are produced at the ends of twigs.

## LOWER BARK

Compared with younger bark, the older bark of the lower trunk is loose and flaking. In trees such as the Scotch pine, older branches tend to fall off, leaving the lower trunk bare.

13

# POWERED BY THE SUN

**L**ike all plants, conifers grow by capturing the energy in sunlight. They use the energy to make new living tissues, including their seeds.

## PHOTOSYNTHESIS

The process of harnessing light energy for growth is known as photosynthesis. The light energy is used to combine water with carbon dioxide to make substances called sugars, which are the plant's food. Photosynthesis also makes oxygen, which is released into the air. This is very useful to animals that need to breathe oxygen to stay alive.

*GREEN LEAVES*

*Only the green leaves of a conifer (above) carry out photosynthesis to produce food. The branches, trunk, and roots (right) obtain their food from leaves through the phloem tubes.*

## PHOTOSYNTHESIS

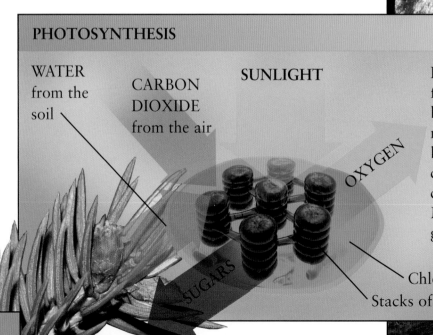

WATER from the soil

CARBON DIOXIDE from the air

SUNLIGHT

OXYGEN

SUGARS

Photosynthesis uses carbon dioxide from the air and water taken up by the roots. It occurs in the microscopic cells of leaves, in tiny button-shaped parts known as chloroplasts. Light is trapped by colored substances called pigments. Most of these, like chlorophyll, are green, which gives plants their color.

Chloroplast
Stacks of thylakoid discs inside chloroplast

*A close view (left) of leaves from a Chinese fir (inset) shows tiny holes, called stomata, on their surface. They allow air to pass in and out of the leaf, bringing in carbon dioxide and taking away oxygen. This is called the gas exchange.*

## NEW GROWTH

Conifers use the energy from sugars to create wood, leaves, cones, and other plant parts from minerals taken in from the soil through the roots. This growth occurs mainly during warmer conditions in the spring or summer. The growth almost stops in the winter.

### LIFE ON THE EDGE

*Conifer leaves have adapted to survive low temperatures and high winds, such as on a mountainside.*

### OUTER LAYERS (HYPODERMIS)

*The cuticle is thick and waxy, to prevent water loss and damage by frost, snow, and wind. Tiny holes, stomata, allow air in so the leaf can obtain carbon dioxide for photosynthesis.*

### MIDDLE LAYERS (MESOPHYLL)

*These are the main sites for cells to carry out photosynthesis. The oxygen they give off passes out through the stomata.*

### VASCULAR BUNDLE

*This bundle of tiny tubes is an extension of the tube network in the trunk. Xylem tubes bring water and minerals from the roots, while phloem takes away the sap containing sugar-rich foods.*

*INSIDE A CONIFER NEED LE (LEAF)*

Epidermis

Cuticle

Xylem

Phloem

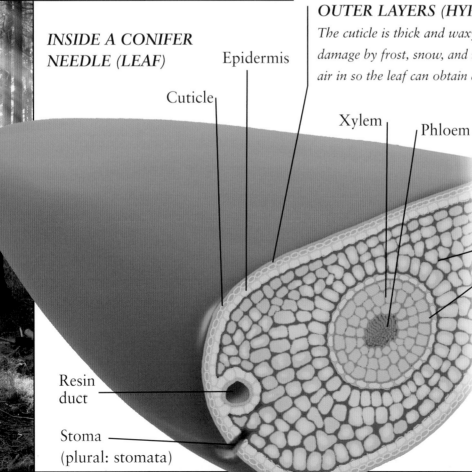

Resin duct

Stoma (plural: stomata)

# CONES AND SEEDS

**C**onifers are named after their cones. These are the reproductive parts that the plant uses to make new seeds.

## MALE AND FEMALE

There are two kinds of cones—male and female. Cones are also known as strobili. They are equivalent to the flowers or blossoms of flowering plants. Most conifers are monoecious, which means they have both female and male cones on the same tree. A few species are dioecious, which means the two types of cones are on different trees. In those cases, the trees themselves are either female or male.

### FLOWERING CONE?

*Some cones, such as the pink pine-flower, resemble the blooms of true flowering plants. But their structure is very different.*

### TWO SEXES

*Like most conifers, the Japanese cedar is monoecious. In most species, the male cones (microstrobili) are smaller and light-colored (above, lower cones). Female cones (megastrobili) are usually larger and greenish when young.*

### THE UNUSUAL YEW

Yews are unusual among conifers because they have berries instead of hard, woody cones. Each berry is a modified cone with a single scale, known as an aril, that has become soft and fleshy. It is open at one end and contains a single seed.

*Yew berries taste sweet and are eaten by many birds. The tough seeds are not digested and pass out in the birds' droppings.*

## MATURING CONES

As female cones (right) mature, they become darker, tougher, and more woody. It may take several years for the seeds to develop fully.

### CONIFER SEEDS

Many conifer seeds have lightweight "wings" (above) that help them blow in the wind and find a suitable place to grow. Pine seeds are known as pine nuts.

### POLLEN COUNTS

Young male cones of the lodgepole pine release clouds of tiny pollen grains that drift away in the wind. Transferring male pollen to a plant's female parts is known as pollination. All conifers are wind-pollinated.

## CONE DEVELOPMENT

Cones grow from buds, which are usually at the ends of twigs. The young cone from an opened bud is sometimes called a cone flower, but it is not a true flower. The male cones release dustlike pollen grains that contain the male sex cells. These cells are carried by the wind to female cones. The male cells join with the female sex cells to start the development of seeds.

### FIRE SEEDS

Some female cones open their scales to release the seeds when they reach a certain age or when they dry out. The lodgepole pinecone does so when it gets very hot, such as during a forest fire. This means the seeds may fall to the ground where other plants have burned away, giving them a better chance to grow.

T he biggest areas of conifer forests are near the top of the world on the lands bordering the frozen Arctic.

### TOUGH TREES

Northern forests cover more land than any other habitat. The most northerly parts of the forests, which give way to treeless regions called tundras, are known as the taiga. A few broad-leaved trees survive here, such as birch, willow, and aspen, but the vast majority are conifers.

### FROZEN SOLID

*Most life shuts down during the long northern winter. Conifer trees become dormant (inactive).*

### *SUBALPINE FIR*

*In North America, fir trees grow next to the tree line where the tundra starts. They are also found on mountains farther south, such as California's Trinity Alps.*

### *SHORT SUMMER*

*In late spring, the snow has barely melted in the taiga. The evergreen leaves begin to capture sunlight for growth. The dark and cold will return in less than four months.*

## NOOTKA CYPRESS

Also known as Alaskan cedar (even though it is not a cedar), the Nootka cypress reaches heights of 130 feet (40 m). It is most common in northwest North America, where some specimens are 1,800 years old.

## FOR THE BIRDS

Cones are very tough and contain little nourishment, but the seeds in female cones are packed with nutrients. Many animals, from beetles to deer and squirrels, have ways to get inside.

*Crossbills (above) have a beak with crossed-over tips, which is adapted to pry open the cone scales and pull out the seeds. Game birds, such as black grouse (right), peck at the seeds and buds to open them. In the spring, they eat the pollen from male cones.*

## WITHSTANDING COLD

Conifers have several adaptations to survive long, cold, snowy winters. Their branches slope downward, allowing snow to slide off. Otherwise the snow would collect and become so heavy that the branches would snap. The thin, tough leaves lose hardly any water and are not damaged even if frozen solid. The bark, however, can collect ice and flake off.

### JACK PINES

*Jack pines often grow in twisted shapes (left). They can be quite small—sometimes less than 16 feet (5 m) tall. Female jack pinecones (above left) may stay closed with their seeds for several years, until a fire's heat opens them.*

19

Conifers are often found in harsh and even extreme habitats, including cold mountaintops and windy, salt-sprayed coasts.

## WINDBREAKERS

Adaptations to extreme cold help conifers survive in places where there are drying winds and little rain. One of these adaptations is sunken stomata. These tiny holes in the leaves that allow in air are set deep in grooves or folds of the leaf. This arrangement prevents wind from blowing away too much moisture from inside the leaf. Shoreline conifers are popular as windbreaks.

### MONTEREY CYPRESS

*The Monterey cypress is common in many parks and gardens, but it only grows naturally along part of the coast in California, where it is protected by law.*

## CEDAR OF LEBANON

*The Lebanon or Lebanese cedar, with its thick, strong branches (right), is featured on the national flag of Lebanon.*

The Lebanese cedar *Cedrus libani* is a popular tree in many regions. Up to 130 feet (40 m) high, it has branches that form a spreading, often flat-topped crown. It originally came from coasts and mountains near the Mediterranean Sea.

## MAJESTIC SCENERY

Conifers are part of the beautiful scenery in places such as southeast Alaska. They can grow among the rocky crags and ridges of the mountains, where the winds are intense and heavy rains regularly wash away the thin soil.

## BLUE SPRUCE

*A blue spruce* Picea pungens *cone opens its scales to release the seeds. This spruce grows in mountains at heights of 10,000 feet (3,000 m).*

## HEMLOCKS AND FIRS

*Hemlocks (above) are noted for their deeply grooved bark and spiral, slightly flattened leaves. They need more moisture than many other conifers and are usually found near river valleys. The Pacific silver fir* Abies amabilis *(right) also needs plenty of moisture and thrives mainly in the cool rain forests of North America's northwest coast.*

## PINE PEST

Pinus pinaster *(right) were taken from their home in southwest Europe and planted in several other areas. In South Africa, it survives too well and has become a pest in that region.*

21

# HOT AND DRY LANDS

Some conifers survive in extreme cold, while others thrive in hot, dry climates. The features that help them through cold winters also work for hot summers.

## SAVING WATER

In the far north, the ground is frozen for part of the year. Tree roots cannot take up any water because it is solid ice. This is a form of drought—a lack of water. Conifers have adapted to such situations.

In hot regions, there is also a lack of water because it hardly ever rains. Conifers are often the only trees that can survive the drought conditions. However, the lack of nutrients in the thin soil means that dry-land conifers grow very slowly, perhaps as little as 4 inches (10 cm) every hundred years.

### DESERT JUNIPER
*Utah junipers (above) can withstand the scorching summer sun and bare rocky lands of southwest North America. There are about 70 kinds of junipers. Most produce female cones that ripen as blue berries that contain one or two seeds. Many animals eat these berries, including desert rats and jackrabbits.*

### PINYONS
*Most pinyon pines have two-needle leaves, and both needles grow from the same place on the twig (left). Some bear single-needle leaves (above left, inset).*

## BALKAN PINE

*Also called Macedonian pine, Pinus peuce (left) is found on otherwise bare hillsides in the Balkans region of southeastern Europe. Its needle leaves are in clumps of five (below).*

## PONDEROSA PINES

The ponderosa pine grows across western North America, where it is known by local names such as Washoe pine, yellow pine, and bull pine. It is an important timber tree in other places, especially Argentina, and it provides many kinds of creatures with food and shelter.

*Ponderosa pines can tolerate dry soil. They are well used by many animals, including the Albert's squirrel (below left) and birds ranging from the goldfinch (below center) to the red-headed woodpecker.*

## CANARY ISLAND PINE

Pinus canariensis *copes with a yearly rainfall of less than 8 inches (20 cm). It covers hills on the Canary Islands of the East Atlantic, off the coast of northwest Africa, and can survive intense wildfires.*

# CONIFER SWAMPS

**S**ome conifers are at home in swamps, marshes, and bogs—places where other trees would suffer from waterlogged roots and trunks.

## LACK OF OXYGEN

One common wetland conifer is the swamp cypress *Taxodium distichum*. It is well known in Mississippi and the Florida Everglades in the south-eastern United States.

A problem for swamp trees is obtaining enough oxygen for their roots in the warm, low-oxygen water. Some conifers have aerial roots, growths from the roots called pneumatophores. They take in oxygen from the air. In the swamp cypress, these growths give the tree a firm base in the soft mud.

### AERIAL ROOTS

*Rounded growths from pond cypress roots, known as "cypress knees," may help the tree stay upright in the shifting silt and mud. They also help take in oxygen, which is scarce in the water.*

### CYPRESS SWAMP

*The swamp cypress' aerial roots (above) are pointed, its cones (left) are round, and its leaves (below) form flat rows. Found across the south-eastern U.S., it is also called the bald cypress because it is deciduous—it loses its leaves in the winter. Some experts say the pond cypress is a kind of swamp cypress. Others suggest it is a different species—*Taxodium ascendens.

## THE TAMARACK

Also called the American larch, the tamarack grows in many places across northern North America, including the wetlands. It is one of the few deciduous conifers.

*Tamaracks grow to about 65 feet (20 m). In the fall, their leaves turn yellow (above). The cones (left) are the smallest of any larch, less than 1 inch (2.5 cm) long.*

## SWAMP WILDLIFE

Swamp cypresses and other wetland conifers are home to many animals. Birds nest in the branches, and wood-boring grubs tunnel into their bark. Fish and freshwater turtles hide among the roots, emerging to feed on fallen leaves and seeds. They also eat worms and other creatures in the still, dark water.

### CREATURES OF THE SWAMP

*In a typical cypress swamp, there may be more than 1,000 species of insects, birds, and other animals. Frogs and other amphibians, such as the spring peeper (1), are especially common. The hermit thrush (2) arrives in winter, white-tailed deer (3) browse around the edge, and pileated woodpeckers (4) search for bark grubs.*

25

# CONIFERS OF THE SOUTH

Conifers are not common in tropical areas around the Equator. But farther south they cover large areas.

## SOUTHERN FAMILIES

More than 200 kinds of conifers grow in South America, southern Africa, Australia, and New Zealand. Many have names taken from northern species, such as spruces and firs. But they are not true members of these groups. They belong to conifer families of southern lands, such as araucarias and podocarps.

### NORFOLK PINE

*Like many other southern "pines," the Norfolk pine is a type of araucaria. It can exceed 200 feet (60 m) in height. Although it is best known on Norfolk Island, near Australia and New Zealand, it has been planted in many other areas because of its size, its straight trunk, and its neat, tidy appearance.*

### CANDELABRA TREE

*The Brazilian araucaria, with leaves at its branch ends, is one of several plants known as candelabra trees.*

### RIMU

*The wood of the podocarp rimu* Dacrydium cupressinum *is highly valued. Once widespread in New Zealand, it is now a protected species.*

### HUGGING THE COAST

*The New Caledonia "pine" is actually a member of the ancient araucaria family of southern conifers. It only grows on the islands of New Caledonia, northeast of Australia.*

## FATHERS OF THE FOREST

The kauris *Agathis* are a subgroup of the araucaria family. There are about 21 species found across southeast Asia, Australia, New Zealand, and the Pacific islands. The huge New Zealand kauris are known traditionally as "fathers of the forest." Their habitats are home to many rare and unusual animals not found anywhere else.

*Kakapo*

New Zealand conifer forests house kiwis (above) and the rare flightless parrot, the kakapo.

### COOK'S ARAUCARIA

Araucaria columnaris, *sometimes called Cook's pine, is from the New Caledonia region. It has a tall, thin, tapering shape and is popular as a park tree, especially in Hawaii (above).*

The New Zealand kauri (above) has a wide, straight trunk, unusual dagger-shaped leaves, and large seed cones (left).

# UNUSUAL CONIFERS

**M**ost conifers are trees, bear cones, have needlelike leaves, and are evergreen. But there are exceptions to all of these features.

### BARE IN WINTER
About a dozen species of larches *Larix* grow across the forests of the far north. Like the few broad-leaved trees in those regions, they are deciduous and lose their leaves in the winter. Other deciduous conifers are the dawn redwood and swamp cypresses.

*Ponderosa pine seed*

*Coulter pine seed*

### WESTERN LARCH
*The pale green leaves of the western larch appear in the spring, darken (right), change to yellow (below), and then drop before winter, leaving the branches (below right).*

### BIG CONE PINE
*The Coulter (big cone pine) has the biggest (but not the longest) cones of any conifer. They are hard, spiny, and 16 inches (40 cm) in length. They weigh more than 9 pounds (4 kg) and produce large seeds (above, compared with other common seeds).*

## POND CYPRESS

*The pond cypress produces lines of new shoots along its twigs and branches in early summer (above). When growing in drier ground, it does not send up the rounded knees from its roots (left).*

## CONIFER BONSAI

The technique of growing miniature trees is known as bonsai. Various conifers can be used, including Japanese white pine and black pine. The tree is carefully shaped over many years to look pleasing to the eye and perhaps resemble its full-sized shape.

*Bonsai methods include removing some of the leaves at particular times, pruning selected shoots and twigs, wrapping wire or putting clamps around the trunk or certain branches, and using pots of special sizes and shapes.*

## REGENERATION

*Several types of conifers can grow again after disasters, such as fires or floods. The pitch pine (left) grows shoots called epicormic sprouts that grow into new twigs after a fire. As a fallen Western hemlock rots (right), it provides nutrients for a new tree.*

29

# GINKGOS AND GNETUMS

The ginkgo (maidenhair tree) and the smaller, herblike gnetums are cousins of conifers. They are within the same group—the "naked seed" gymnosperms.

## THE MISSING LINK

*Ginkgo biloba* is the only remaining member of an ancient group of gymnosperms and is often called a living fossil. Its family, Ginkgoaceae, was once far more common and widespread. Originally from the Zhejiang area of China, it is now planted around the world in parks and gardens and along roads.

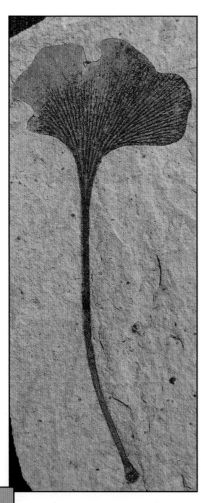

*FOSSILS*

*The distinct fan-shaped leaves, cones, and seeds of ginkgos date back more than 200 million years.*

### GINKGO "FLOWERS"

*In the spring, the male ginkgo tree's new cones look like flowers. As in conifers, they release clouds of pollen grains. These blow in the wind to the acorn-shaped ovules of female trees.*

## TWO SEXES

The ginkgo tree can reach about 165 feet (50 m) in height in good growing conditions. It is dioecious, and the male trees grow pollen cones. Female trees have twig-tip ovules that mature into fleshy fruits.

### VARIED LEAVES

*No two ginkgo leaves have the same shape, even on the same stem (left). Gingkos are deciduous, and their leaves turn yellow and drop in the fall (above left).*

## TRADITIONAL USES

The ginkgo became known to
Western science in the 1690s when
travelers brought it to Europe.
Various parts are used in traditional
Chinese medicine, usually powdered (above) or ground into
paste. The leaves (top) are said to help digestive problems,
and the seeds are taken for energy or as a tonic.

## FRUITS AND SEEDS

The name ginkgo is said to
come from an ancient word
meaning "silver apricot." The
fruits (below) resemble small
apricots or plums and have a
shiny covering. The seeds
(left) are used to treat
digestive and
skin conditions.

## GNETUMS

Gnetums, such as *Gnetum gnemon*,
are a small group of evergreen
gymnosperms in the tropics.
There are about 35 species. Some
resemble trees and shrubs, while
others look like herbs and grow
as vines.

The common
gnetum is from east and
southeast Asia and the
Pacific islands. It is a
small tree with conelike strobili that
mature into yellow or reddish fruits
that are about 1 inch (2.5 cm) long.

# CYCADS

Close relatives of the conifers, cycads flourished millions of years ago, covering huge areas. Their numbers have since gone down.

## TROPICAL HABITS

Cycads are often mistaken for palm trees, ferns, tree-ferns, or even pineapples. Most live in the tropics and subtropics. More than 300 species are known so far, but these gymnosperms have not been thoroughly studied by scientists. There may be more to be identified. Most types are evergreen and have a stout woody trunk with a crown of large, frond-shaped leaves, like a stumpy palm tree.

### AUSTRALIAN CYCAD

*The MacDonnell Ranges cycad (above), about 7 feet (2 m) tall, grows in hills with the same name in the Northern Territory of Australia. It is a harsh habitat with rocky slopes, hot sun, and long dry periods.*

### REPRODUCTIVE PARTS

Cycas revoluta, *sometimes known as the sago palm, is really the sago cycad. Its male reproductive parts are like conifer cones, growing upright on the trunk top (left). The female parts are more flowerlike (above) and are on separate plants from the cones.*

Wood's cycads are grown by cuttings (vegetative propagation), a form of asexual reproduction. All of the plants are male clones with the same genes.

*Encephalartos woodii*, also called Wood's cycad, from Africa is among the world's rarest wild plants. It is thought to have completely died out in the wild. These cycads are kept in parks and gardens. They must be bred by cuttings because no female plants are known.

## TWO SAGOS

The starchy flour called sago—from the true sago palm Metroxylon sagu (right)—is a common food in southeast Asia. It is often cooked as pancakes. The sago cycad, however, is not edible. All of its parts are poisonous, especially the seeds. It causes severe illness and even death in people, pets, and farm animals.

## SAGO SEEDING

Sago cycad seeds take from six to 12 months to mature in the female cone (right). When ripe, they are about the size of walnuts. They sprout into green-shooted seedlings (below).

## STANGERIA

The cycad Stangeria *from South Africa has* an underground trunk like a big carrot, large leaves (above right), and stalked cones (above left).

# RECORD BREAKERS

Conifers are among the tallest, heaviest, oldest, and fastest-growing living things on Earth.

### MEGA-TREES

The world's largest tree is a conifer known as General Sherman, a giant sequoia growing in California. With a height of 275 feet (85 meters), the sequoia is thought to be 2,500 years old. The trunk measures 36 feet (11 m) around at the base. Its estimated weight is more than 6,000 tons (5,400 metric tons), which is 30 times as heavy as the world's biggest animal, the blue whale.

*OLDEST LIVING THINGS*

*Yew trees (above) can live to be 1,000 years old. Bristlecone pines from west and southwest North America (below) are almost 5,000 years old. Some Norway spruces, or* Picea abies, *are even older, at 9,550 years.*

*MASSIVE CONIFERS*

*The General Sherman tree,* Sequoiadendron giganteum *(above), grows in Sequoia National Park. It is visited by thousands of people every year. The tallest trees include the coast redwoods* Sequoia sempervirens, *like those in Redwood National Park, California (above left).*

*On average, the widest tree trunks belong to the Montezuma cypress* Taxodium mucronatum *(left).*

## TALLEST TREES

Coast redwoods hold the record for the tallest living things, with some exceeding 380 feet (115 m). Coast Douglas firs and Sitka spruces also reach enormous heights of about 320 feet (100 m). The Sitka spruce is named after a city in southeast Alaska.

### THE DAWN REDWOOD—A LIVING FOSSIL

The dawn redwood *Metasequoia glyptostroboides* was once known by scientists only from fossils— remains or impressions of plants or animals that have hardened into rock. However, living specimens were discovered in southwest China in 1941.

*Once known only from fossils (left), dawn redwoods (right) are now grown widely around the world.*

*GREATEST FORESTS*

*The world's largest unbroken areas of trees, known as the boreal forests, stretch across the northern parts of North America, Europe, and Asia. The forests contain a mixture of conifer species.*

# FORESTS AND PLANTATIONS

**S**ome of the world's biggest farms are tree farms—conifer plantations where trees are grown by the millions.

## BIG BUSINESS

Growing timber is one of the world's largest industries. Conifers make up more than 99 percent of trees. Each day, one person can plant more than 1,500 trees. Hundreds of millions of conifers are planted to replace those that are cut down.

## TIMBER PRODUCTION

*Conifers begin their forestry lives as seeds in greenhouses, where conditions are arranged for them to germinate quickly into seedlings, like those of ponderosa pines (above). At a certain age or size, the seedlings are transferred outside into nursery areas. They are put into*

*rows where they grow into saplings (above). The next stage may be to move the saplings out into the main plantation areas. As the trees reach a suitable height*

*for a particular use, they are cut down by loggers or powerful tree harvesters (left). In clearcutting, all the trees are cut down (top), which is the opposite of selective logging.*

## PLANTATION STOCK

*Some of the most common conifers in plantations are Douglas firs Pseudotsuga (right), with drooping female cones about 4 inches (10 cm) in length (below). Found originally in coastal areas of western North America, they are now raised across Europe, South America, and New Zealand. Tall and fast-growing, they are often the most productive of all timber trees.*

## CONIFER BENEFITS

Conifers have several advantages over broad-leaved trees. They are easier to handle, they grow faster, and they can be raised in harsh habitats with poor soil, where broad-leaved trees would not thrive. They also have straighter trunks that are easier to cut and prepare by machine.

## THE OLD LOG CABIN

One of the great symbols of the pioneering times is the log cabin. It could be built in a few days with nothing more than an axe and saw. Wood is an excellent insulator, keeping heat in and cold out.

*Log cabins are well-known in North America, but they originated in northern Europe. Even the shingles are made of wood.*

## TRANSPORTATION

*In areas with plenty of rain and rivers, millions of logs can float from the plantations to mills downstream.*

# CONIFER TIMBERS

## SAWMILLS

*Sawmills, also called lumber mills, are often along rivers, where the freshly cut trees with their branches trimmed off can be floated. Other mills are near railroads or highways.*

Certain types of conifers produce certain kinds of timber, each suited to specific uses and products.

## SOFTWOODS AND HARDWOODS

Conifer timbers are usually called softwoods. This is to distinguish them from hardwoods, which come from broad-leaved trees, such as maple, beech, hickory, oak, and teak. However, not all softwoods are soft. Siberian larch is harder than many hardwoods, while the hardwood balsa is very light and soft.

### KILN DRYING

*To speed up the natural seasoning process, timber is dried in large ovens called kilns. Seasoning prevents cracking and bending.*

## GOOD YEWS

Long ago, one of the most prized conifers was the yew. Its heartwood was strong, and its sapwood was bendy and elastic—an ideal combination for making the longbows that helped decide several wars in medieval times.

*European yew* Taxus baccata

## CUT TO SIZE

In most sawmills, the trunks of cut trees are looked at for their species, size, quality, and knotting (where branches joined the trunk). The trunks go in at one end, are cut by a variety of power saws, and emerge as lumber that is cut to specific sizes.

## LONGLEAF PINE

*The longleaf pine Pinus palustris has an especially resistant timber prized for its long-lasting quality. The trees (left) can grow up to 115 feet (35 m). They have long needles, and the female cones (above) take up to two years to ripen. The timber has been used for projects such as flooring and decking, in which the wood has to stand up to wear and tear. Another quality of the longleaf pine is its resistant to fire, making it valuable for building bridges (above). It is the official state tree of Alabama.*

## EASY CARVING

*Each conifer wood has its own features, such as the quality of grain (direction of wood fibers). Japanese red cedar is traditionally used for furniture in temples.*

*Pacific yew bark*

Some yews have many uses. An anti-cancer drug was prepared from the bark of the Pacific yew of coastal northwest North America. Chinese yew is used to make wooden shoes and bed frames.

*Leaves of Pacific yew*
*Taxus brevifolia*

*A bow made from a single piece of European yew*

# CONIFER PRODUCTS

Conifers supply us with more than timber. They are harvested and processed into hundreds of substances and items.

## KITCHENS AND CHEMICALS

Pine nuts are used to give flavor to pesto, a type of sauce. A sugar substitute can be produced from the sugar pine. Western hemlock is used in the leather industry. Canada balsam, a thick liquid from the balsam fir, is part of an invisible glue used to fix lenses in telescopes and microscopes.

*PAPER*
*One of the main uses for conifer wood (above) is making paper. The wood is*

*treated with chemicals and mashed into pulp to free the fibers. The mixture is then laid out as long sheets on a conveyor belt. From there they are pressed and dried into long rolls (above, inset).*

*NUTRITIOUS NUTS*
*Several kinds of conifer seeds are noted for their taste, nourishing content, and medical uses. Pinyon nuts (above far left) can be ground into a soup. Stone pine nuts (above) give flavor to pesto and hummus (above right). Korean pine nuts from the female cones (right) are the most widespread.*

# WRITING AND WORSHIPPING

Although plastic pens are common, about 40 million pencils are made every day. The common wood is incense cedar, which has a pleasant scent and splinters little when sharpened. The six-sided shape that prevents rolling was invented by U.S. pencil factory owner Ebenezer Wood in the mid-1800s.

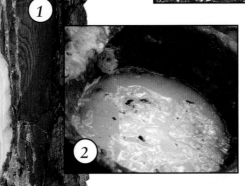

The wood of incense cedar Calocedrus *(top)* is stiff but soft enough to sharpen for pencils *(left)*. It has a spicy fragrance when burned as incense *(above)*.

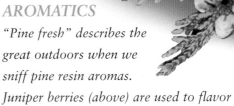

## AROMATICS

*"Pine fresh" describes the great outdoors when we sniff pine resin aromas. Juniper berries (above) are used to flavor drinks, and juniper and other conifer woods are burned as incense in Buddhist temples.*

## RESIN

*The sticky resin from conifer trees has had many uses in the past. Collected by tapping trees (left), it was used as pitches, tars, and similar substances for building wooden ships. A tree is tapped by cutting the bark (1) so the resin drips into a container (2). Purified liquid resins are used to make inks, paper, paints, varnishes, cements, sealants, glues, waxes, and chewing gum. Solid rosin (3), a resin often used in making varnish, is rubbed onto the strings of violins, cellos, and similar stringed instruments.*

**1**

**2**

**3**

# CONIFER CONSERVATION

**I**n some conifer forests and plantations, trees stretch over the horizon. But not all types of conifers are in plentiful supply.

## PROBLEMS

Some conifer species, such as the Florida torreya, are very rare. It is endangered because of fungus diseases. There are only a few thousand left. Other conifers are much more common because they have been taken to new regions and planted for timber. These species take over natural habitats and threaten the local plants and animals.

*ALMOST GONE?*
*Florida torreya Torreya taxifolia (top and inset) survives in the wild in a few places on the Florida-Georgia border. Its strong smell has led to such nicknames as "stinking cedar." Some are raised in the Appalachian Mountains. There are plans to plant wild seedlings north of the mountain range to save the species.*

*INVADERS*
*Some plantation conifers are invasive species. They are moved from commercial forests as seedlings and take over the natural trees and other vegetation, as in New Zealand (left). The Aleppo pine (above), originally from the Mediterranean region, is a "tree weed" in South Australia.*

# CONIFER DISEASES

Some conifers suffer greatly from diseases caused by insect pests, fungi or molds, and microbes such as bacteria. In plantations where all the trees are the same species and close together, a disease can spread in just a few years and wipe out the entire crop. Conifers also act as carriers of diseases that spread to affect other plants.

## ANNOSUS

*A common disease of conifers is Annosus butt-rot (above), where the fungus* Fomes annosus *attacks the tree's butt—the lowest part of the trunk at ground level. Other diseases include brown-spot needle blight, Brunchorstia dieback, and charcoal root disease.*

## NEEDLECAST

*Some fungal infections cause conifers' leaves to discolor and fall, an effect known as needlecast.*

## WOLLEMI PINE

*Wild trees are protected by law. Their natural habitat is a guarded secret.*

The Wollemi pine *Wollemia nobilis* is not a true pine. It is a type of araucaria. It has long been known from its fossils. In 1994 park ranger David Noble found living trees in a steep valley near Sydney, Australia. This "living fossil" is endangered in the wild, but it is being bred and exported worldwide.

*"Save the Wollemi" involves selling plants raised from cuttings.*

## PESTS

*Among the most infamous conifer pests are spruce budworms (above). They are caterpillars of small* Choristoneura *moths. They devour young leaves, buds, and the soft parts of spruces, firs, and other conifers (right). The mountain pine beetle* Dendroctonus *(below) burrows in the bark of limber, lodgepole, and other pines.*

43

# CLASSIFICATION OF LIFE

Scientists classify living things depending on how their features and the parts inside them compare with other living things. Coniferous plants (gymnosperms) share features, such as making naked seeds—those not in fruits. But there are many groups, from delicate bushes to massive trees. Their similarities and differences show how conifers have changed and evolved around the world over millions of years.

The main groups of living things are known as domains. The next groups are usually kingdom, phylum (division), class, order, family, genus, and species. To see how this system works, follow the example on page 45 of how the Scotch pine tree *Pinus sylvestris* is classified in the division Coniferae (Pinophyta).

## BIOLOGICAL CLASSIFICATION: DOMAINS

### BACTERIA

Single-celled prokaryotes, found in most places on Earth

### ARCHAEA

Single-celled prokaryotes, many surviving in extreme conditions

### EUKARYA

#### KINGDOMS

PROTISTA: Single-celled eukaryotes, with some simple multicelled forms

FUNGI: Multicelled life-forms that digest their food externally

PLANTAE: Multicelled life-forms that obtain energy by photosynthesis

ANIMALIA: Multicelled life-forms that get their energy by taking in food

# GROUPS OF CONIFERS

The main Coniferae group is split into between six and 10 groups known as divisions. The groups below are seven families of conifers.

Pinaceae
Araucariaceae
Podocarpaceae
Sciadopityaceae
Cupressaceae
Cephalotaxaceae
Taxaceae

Scotch pine is a very widespread conifer. Originally found in Northern Europe, it is now planted in North America and many other regions.

**DOMAIN:** Eukarya

**KINGDOM:** Plantae

**DIVISION:** Coniferae (Pinophyta)

**CLASS:** Pinopsida

**ORDER:** Pinales

**FAMILY:** Pinaceae

**GENUS:** *Pinus*

**SPECIES:** *sylvestris*

Pinus sylvestris *(Scotch pine)*

# GLOSSARY

**BARK**
Hard, woody, outer layer of a large plant, such as a bush, shrub, or tree; gives protection against physical damage, diseases, and pests, and slows down water loss

**BOREAL FOREST**
Areas of unbroken forest across the northern regions of North America, Europe, and Asia; contains mostly conifer trees

**CAMBIUM**
Thin layer of rapidly multiplying microscopic cells in a shoot, stem, root, or similar plant part; makes other parts and tissues

**CELL**
Tiniest basic unit, the "building block" of life; some microscopic living things, such as bacteria and most protists, are just one cell each; larger plants and animals are made of billions of cells

**CHLOROPHYLL**
Green substance that captures light energy to carry out photosynthesis

**CHLOROPLAST**
Tiny part inside a living cell that contains the substances needed to capture light energy and carry out photosynthesis

**CONES**
Parts of a conifer plant specialized for reproduction or breeding; also called strobili

**DIOECIOUS**
Plant species that has female reproductive parts, such as cones, on one plant and male reproductive parts on another; each plant is either male or female

**EUKARYOTE**
Cell that has an outer cell membrane and other membranes inside, enclosing parts such as the nucleus

**GERMINATION**
When a plant seed, spore, or similar part starts to grow after reaching good conditions of light, moisture, and nutrients

**GYMNOSPERMS**
Large group of seed-making plants in which the seeds are unenclosed; gymnosperms include conifers, cycads, gnetums, and ginkgos

**HYPODERMIS**
Outer layers of a conifer needle, including the cuticle and stomata

**INVASIVE SPECIES**
Plant or animal species that has been introduced into an ecosystem

**MESOPHYLL**
Middle layers of a conifer needle or similar leaf, including the mesophyll cells that carry out photosynthesis

**MONOECIOUS**
Plant species that has separate female and male reproductive parts, such as cones, on the same plant

**PHLOEM**
Long, microscopic, tubelike vessels that carry energy-rich nutrients made in the leaves to all other parts of a plant

**PHOTOSYNTHESIS**
Capturing light energy to join simple substances and create food, which is used to grow, develop, and carry out life processes

**POLLEN**
Tiny grains made by the male parts of a plant; pollen contains the male sex cells (gametes) for reproduction; they often look like yellow or pale-colored dust

## POLLINATION
Transfer of a plant's male pollen grains to the female reproductive parts of a plant of the same kind; in conifers, this almost always occurs by wind

## STOMATA
Microscopic holes in the surface of a leaf, usually on the underside; they allow air to pass in and out of the leaf, bringing in carbon dioxide for photosynthesis and taking away oxygen

## PROKARYOTE
Cell that has a membrane covering but no other separate membranes inside, so it lacks membrane-enclosed parts, such as a nucleus

## VASCULAR BUNDLES
Groups of specialized tubelike structures inside some plants; includes phloem and xylem vessels, which transport water, sap, and other fluids within the plant body

## XYLEM
Long, microscopic, tubelike vessels that carry water and dissolved minerals absorbed by the roots to all parts of the plant, especially the leaves

Look for all the books in this series:

*Cocci, Spirilla & Other Bacteria*
*Ferns, Mosses & Other Spore-Producing Plants*
*Molds, Mushrooms & Other Fungi*
*Protozoans, Algae & Other Protists*
*Redwoods, Hemlocks & Other*
 *Cone-Bearing Plants*
*Sunflowers, Magnolia Trees & Other*
 *Flowering Plants*

# FURTHER RESOURCES

## FURTHER READING
Bash, Barbara. *Ancient Ones: The World of the Old-Growth Douglas Fir*. San Francisco: Sierra Book Club for Kids, 2002.

Burnie, David. *Tree*. New York: DK Publishing, 2005.

Ingoglia, Gina. *The Tree Book for Kids and Their Grown Ups*. Brooklyn, N.Y.: Brooklyn Botanic Garden, 2008.

Stewart, Melissa. *Classification of Life*. Minneapolis: Twenty-First Century Books, 2008.

## INTERNET SITES
FactHound offers a safe, fun way to find Internet sites related to this book. All of the sites on FactHound have been researched by our staff.

Here's all you do:
Visit *www.facthound.com*
FactHound will fetch the best sites for you!

# INDEX